The Balance Beam

Navigating Life's Divine Harmony

The Balance Beam

Navigating Life's Divine Harmony

By:
Fr Kyrillos Farag

ST SHENOUDA PRESS
SYDNEY, AUSTRALIA
2024

The Balance Beam
Navigating Life's Divine Harmony

By: Fr Kyrillos Farag

COPYRIGHT © 2024
St. Shenouda Press

All rights reserved. Except for brief quotations in critical publications or reviews, no part of this book may be reproduced in any manner without prior written permission from the publisher.

ST SHENOUDA PRESS
8419 Putty Rd,
Putty, NSW, 2330
Sydney, Australia
www.stshenoudapress.com

ISBN 13: 978-0-6457704-6-9

All scripture quotations, unless otherwise indicated, are taken from the New King James Version®. Copyright © 1982 by Thomas Nelson, Inc. Used by permission. All rights reserved

Dedication

To the Blessed the Ever Virgin Mary, Mother of God and Mother of Humanity, Whose unwavering faith, grace, and love Serve as a guiding light for young families, May her example inspire us to navigate life's complexities with courage, wisdom, and unwavering devotion. In her embrace, we find solace and strength, guiding us to discover the divine harmony that lies within the tapestry of our lives.

With profound gratitude and reverence, this book is lovingly dedicated to Saint Mary, the Mother of God and Mother of Salvation

Remember us before the throne of God that He may forgive us our sins.

14 August, 2023
Saint Mary Fast

Acknowledgments and Gratitude

"I would like to extend my sincere gratitude to several remarkable individuals whose contributions were instrumental in shaping this book.

First and foremost, I want to express my deepest appreciation to Fr. Matthew Attia. His invaluable advice, unwavering support, and profound wisdom have been a guiding light throughout this journey. His insights into the spiritual aspects of the book have enriched its content and made it more meaningful.

I am also profoundly grateful to Dr Wagdy Samir for his meticulous editing of the book. His patience, keen eye for detail, and brilliant ideas have polished the manuscript, making it more cohesive and reader-friendly.

Additionally, I extend my heartfelt thanks to Mrs Michelle Tanious, a seasoned professional in clinical psychology and counselling. Her time spent reading the book and sharing feedback from her extensive experience have added depth and authenticity to its content.

Each of these individuals has played a pivotal role in elevating this work to its highest potential. Their expertise, generosity, and dedication to this project have left an indelible mark, for which I am truly thankful.

This book stands as a testament to the power of collaboration, and I am humbled and honoured to have had the privilege of working alongside these exceptional individuals. Their contributions have made this book a more meaningful and impactful resource.

Thank you for being a part of this journey and for helping bring this book to fruition."

Table of Contents

PART ONE - HARMONY IN CREATION

Chapter 1 - Seeking the Kingdom — The Path to Balance 3

Chapter 2 - The Artistry of Creation 13

Chapter 3 - Humanity's Unique Role 17

Chapter 4 - The Dance of Day and Night 23

Chapter 5 - Stewardship and Responsibility 29

Chapter 6 - Embracing Diversity 35

Chapter 7 - Lessons from the Animal Kingdom 43

Chapter 8 - Walking in Divine Balance 49

PART TWO - A CHALLENGING WORLD

Chapter 9 - Navigating Challenges in Modern Times 57

Chapter 10 - The Busyness Trap 67

Chapter 11 - Cultural Influences 77

Chapter 12 - Balancing Faith and Practicality 81

Chapter 13 - Finding Balance in the Storm 91

Chapter 14 - The Challenge of Cultivating Love
in a World Lacking Love 97

Chapter 15 - Nurturing Balanced Children in a
Complex World by empowering them 105

PART THREE - NAVIGATING LIFE THROUGH CHRISTIAN VAUES

Chapter 16 - Overcoming the Challenge of Comparisons
in the Light of Christian Values 123

Chapter 17 - Pursuing Wealth in Alignment with
Christian Principles 133

Chapter 18 - Navigating a Technological World with
Christian Wisdom 141

Chapter 19 - Anchoring and Amplifying Christian
Faith in a World of Shifting Sands 151

Chapter 20 - Nurturing a Strong Christian Family in
Today's World 161

Chapter 21 - Embracing Purity in Christian Living
for Young Families 171

Chapter 22 - Embracing Unselfishness in Young
Christian Families 181

Chapter 23 - Balancing Focus on the Kingdom of
God in Young Families 195

Chapter 24 - Allocating Time to God in the Lives
of Young Christian Families 203

Chapter 25 - Navigating Identity Challenges in Christian Families 209

Chapter 26 - Embracing Contentment and Establishing Priorities for a Balanced Life 217

Chapter 27 - Unveiling Your Life's Purpose: Crafting a Symphony of Destiny 235

Chapter 28 - The Art of Positive Compromise to Focus on a Few Basic Objectives 241

Chapter 29 - The Laws of in-laws 253

Chapter 30 - The Pressure of Maintaining Social Image...261

Preface

In "The Balance Beam: Navigating Life's Divine Harmony," young Christian families are invited on a transformative journey of faith, love, and purpose. This book, akin to a tapestry woven with wisdom, stories, and biblical insights, guides families toward living harmoniously in a world filled with challenges.

Coping with everyday life's complex and diverse challenges, which is not an easy task, can upset the balance and harmony we seek. Many good people try hard to maintain balance but sometimes feel overwhelmed and defeated.

The journey begins with the captivating analogy of a gymnast on a balance beam—an elegant display of poise and precision. Just as Simone Biles Owens, the most decorated gymnast in the history of the gymnastics world, masterfully conquers the balance beam, young families are encouraged to master the art of balance in various aspects of life. The book encompasses a range of themes, all interwoven with spiritual depth and practical wisdom.

From embracing contentment and establishing Christ-centred priorities to nurturing strong relationships and finding purpose, the chapters are designed to empower families to navigate the complexities of modern life. The message is clear: it's possible to harmonise faith, relationships, responsibilities, and aspirations in a way that reflects God's design and purpose in life.

Each chapter is an expedition into a specific facet of life, illuminated by biblical verses, inspiring stories, and the wisdom of early church fathers. "The Balance Beam" isn't just a book; it's a guide for families to navigate the challenges and joys of today's world while holding fast to their Christian values.

As families grapple with challenges like technology, comparisons, and pursuing wealth, the book offers guidance rooted in Scripture. It reinforces the importance of love, service, and humility in the faith journey with anecdotes from ancient saints to modern-day heroes.

Ultimately, "The Balance Beam" is a call to prioritise God's presence and purpose in every facet of life. It's an invitation to cherish the joyful moments, stand firm in trials, and align with God's divine tapestry. Through the ups and downs, the book reminds us that, like skilled gymnasts on the balance beam, we too can navigate life with grace and confidence, secure in the knowledge that God is our ultimate guide.

In a world often troubled with chaos and confusion, "The Balance Beam" is a resounding affirmation that a life lived in divine harmony is not only possible but deeply rewarding. It's a compass that points young Christian families toward a life of significance, fulfilment, and unwavering faith.

PART ONE

HARMONY IN CREATION

Chapter 1

Seeking the Kingdom – The Path to Balance

Amid the vibrant tapestry of life, where dreams, aspirations, and responsibilities interweave, lies the profound challenge of maintaining an unwavering focus on the Kingdom of God. In the modern world, where distractions abound, and demands tug at our attention, young Christian families find themselves navigating a delicate dance—a dance that requires constant discernment to keep the eternal perspective in view while tending to the temporal.

In Saint Matthew's Gospel, our Lord Jesus Christ imparts a timeless truth that resonates with the hearts of young families seeking balance amidst life's demands: *"But seek first the kingdom of God and His righteousness, and all these things shall be added to you"* (Matthew 6:33 – all scriptural references are from NKJV). These words are not mere counsel; they are a divine roadmap guiding us toward the essence of balance.

Consider the tale of young couple Michael and Sarah. With their hands full of the joys and responsibilities of parenthood, careers, and community involvement, they often find themselves swept up in a whirlwind of busyness. Despite their sincere faith, the cares of life sometimes cloud their vision of the eternal.

One evening, as they sat together reflecting, Michael shared his realisation that their pursuits had been tethered more to the world's rhythm than to the symphony of God's Kingdom. Sarah nodded in agreement, recognising the subtle erosion of their focus on the eternal amid the clamour of the mundane.

Drawing inspiration from Saint Matthew 6:33, they embarked on a transformative journey to recalibrate their priorities. They resolved to prioritise their spiritual growth as a couple and as parents, carving out dedicated time for prayer, scripture reading, and discussions on matters of faith. They chose to volunteer together in Christian community service projects, channelling their energies into tangible expressions of God's love.

As they took deliberate steps to seek the Kingdom first, Michael and Sarah discovered a remarkable phenomenon—their other responsibilities, though not diminished, seemed to fall into place more naturally. The Kingdom-oriented perspective infused new vitality into their daily lives, imbuing ordinary moments with a sense of divine purpose.

Seeking the Kingdom of God: The wisdom of the early church fathers resonates profoundly with this enduring principle. As articulated by St. John Chrysostom, one of the great voices of early Christianity, "The kingdom of God is not defined by food and drink, but by the virtues of righteousness, self-control, and peace" (Homilies on the Gospel of Matthew). These words unearth a fundamental truth that underscores the far-reaching impact of seeking the Kingdom of God. It's not a pursuit limited to specific rituals or practices but a transformative journey that permeates and enriches every facet of our existence.

St. John Chrysostom's insight encourages us to grasp the holistic nature of the Kingdom's pursuit. It's a path that not only shapes our spiritual life within the walls of our church but extends its influence to the realm of our daily interactions, decisions, and character formation. This perspective emphasises that the pursuit of righteousness in aligning our actions with moral integrity and self-control, tempering our desires and impulses, and cultivating harmony within ourselves and our relationships are integral to seeking the Kingdom.

By embracing these virtues, young Christian families strengthen their spiritual journey and become beacons of Christ's teachings to those around them. The pursuit of the Kingdom takes on a dynamic dimension—a ripple effect that extends beyond the individual and familial sphere to touch the lives of colleagues, friends, neighbours, and the wider community.

Thus, the teachings of St. John Chrysostom serve as a poignant reminder that the Kingdom of God is not a remote destination but a transformative way of life that radiates its light through our every action. It reminds us that as we endeavour to balance the demands of daily life with an unwavering focus on the Kingdom, thus contributing to the fabric of a more just, compassionate, and peaceful world.

Balancing the demands of daily life with an unwavering focus on the Kingdom of God is undoubtedly a challenge, yet it is a challenge laden with immeasurable rewards. Like Michael and Sarah, young families can choose to intentionally elevate the eternal above the temporal. In seeking the Kingdom, they discover that true balance is not a precarious act of juggling but a harmonious rhythm that uplifts their journey, infusing every stride with the enduring light of God's purpose.

So, dear readers, as you navigate the intricate choreography of life, remember the profound truth: *"Seek first the Kingdom of God,"* and all other aspects shall fall into place. Let this principle guide your steps, keeping your gaze fixed on the eternal while tending to the present and infusing your family's journey with the radiant melody of divine harmony.

Why the Balance Beam? In the captivating world of gymnastics, the balance beam stands as both a stage and a crucible, demanding an exquisite fusion of poise, precision, and unwavering focus. A focused journey perfected by American artistic gymnast Simone Biles Owens. Her seven Olympic medals, tied with Shannon Miller for the most Olympic medals won by an American gymnast, is the equal ninth-most overall. Having won 25 World Championship medals, she is the most decorated gymnast in the history of the Gymnastics World Championships, conquering the beam's delicate equilibrium; gymnasts mesmerise us with their grace and determination. Beyond the dazzling routines and the thunderous applause lies a profound lesson—a lesson that resonates not only within the gymnastics arena but also throughout the intricate fabric of life itself.

Imagine the scene—the hushed anticipation as a gymnast steps onto the beam, a slender strip of wood raised just inches above the ground. The air is filled with a palpable tension—a tension that mirrors the challenges of life itself. With every step, every turn, and every leap, the gymnast must balance her body's movements with the beam's unforgiving dimensions. It's a mesmerising blend of athletic prowess and artistic finesse, a metaphor for the journey we all embark upon—a journey that demands a delicate balance of physical, emotional, and spiritual elements.

Simone Biles Owens, a remarkable athlete of extraordinary talent and resilience, has mastered the balance beam and navigated life's intricate journey. Her journey, interwoven with threads of challenges and triumphs, encapsulates the essence of discovering harmony in a world filled with contrasts. While she flawlessly manoeuvres on the beam, she imparts invaluable insights that resonate deeply with young couples embarking on the wondrous voyage of marriage and family.

Through her illustrious career, Simone Biles Owens unveils a truth: balance transcends mere physical equilibrium—it extends far beyond that, encompassing realms of faith, relationships, values, and purpose. It's about unearthing that divine harmony where the various facets of life harmoniously meld into a radiant whole. Every step she takes on the beam becomes a metaphor for the steps we take on life's grand journey—a path that calls for balance, grace, determination, and humility.

Amid the exuberance of success and the shadows of challenges, young Christian families find themselves on their own metaphorical balance beams. Striving to uphold their faith, fulfil their responsibilities, and nurture their relationships, they face the daunting task of harmonising their roles as spouses, parents, individuals, and believers. Just as a gymnast's graceful performance requires a profound understanding of her own body and its limits, young Christian couples must discern the delicate balance between their aspirations, obligations, and the rhythms of daily life.

Committing to the Lord: In this quest for balance, the wisdom of Proverbs 16:3 resonates: *"Commit your works to the Lord, and your thoughts will be established."* Here lies the essence of navigating life's balance beam—to anchor our endeavours, dreams, and decisions in a foundation of faith. It's the acknowledgment that as we seek harmony in our roles and responsibilities, we must ultimately surrender our plans to the Divine Artist who orchestrates the symphony of our lives.

As Simone herself once aptly put it, "If you're having fun, that's when the best memories are built." Within these words, we unearth a philosophy that underpins the core of joy and fulfilment in embracing life's voyage. Whether in moments of exhilarating victory or phases of challenging growth, we're summoned to find joy, for it's within these moments that unforgettable memories are etched—memories that imbue the tapestry of our lives with vibrant hues of experience and significance.

Resting in God: Simone Biles Owens's odyssey isn't confined to the realm of sports; it is also a profound spiritual journey. In the words of the early church father Saint Augustine, "You have made us for yourself, O Lord, and our heart is restless until it rests in you" (Augustine of Hippo). These words give us a glimpse of the eternal truth that our hearts yearn for a deeper connection, a divine harmony that transcends life's temporal rhythm. Amidst the cacophony of the world, Simone's journey resonates with this yearning: a reminder that genuine fulfilment is discovered in the embrace of the Divine.

From a Christian perspective, achieving balance holds paramount importance. The Bible guides us with verses highlighting the significance of harmonising various aspects of life. Ecclesiastes 3:1 reminds us, *"To everything there is a season, a time for every purpose under heaven."* This verse underscores the ebb and flow of life's phases and the need to embrace them with balance and grace.

In the teachings of our Lord Jesus Christ, we find a profound emphasis on balance. He instructs us not to be overly consumed by the worries of life, stating in Matthew 6:33, *"But seek first the kingdom of God and His righteousness, and all these things shall be added to you."* This prioritisation of seeking God's kingdom echoes the essence of finding balance in placing our spiritual alignment before the world's clamour.

Love as a Balancing Act: In the journey of Christian families, balance is pivotal. Balancing the roles of spouse, parent, individual, and believer can be intricate yet fulfilling.

The Apostle Paul provides insight in Ephesians 5:25, directing husbands to *"love your wives, just as Christ also loved the church."* This speaks of the vital balance between selflessness, love, and leadership within a marriage.

Tertullian, an early church father, wisely reminds us, "We ought never to do wrong, except in order that we may do right." This sentiment reflects the heart of balance—striving to find equilibrium in our choices, priorities, and pursuits, always guided by the overarching principle of righteousness.

The Significance of Even Small Matters: Once upon a time, in a bustling village nestled between lush hills and a tranquil river, lived a wise elder named Elias. His presence was known far and wide for his profound insights and the tranquillity radiating from him. People often sought his counsel on matters of life, faith, and balance.

One day, a young villager named Sofia approached Elias with a heavy heart. She had been struggling to juggle her responsibilities as a loving wife, a dedicated mother, a diligent homemaker, and an active member of her church community. The weight of these roles left her feeling overwhelmed as if she were on a teeter-totter that threatened to tip over.

Sofia poured out her heart to Elias, explaining her desire to excel in all her roles while fearing that one wrong step could upset the delicate equilibrium of her life. Elias listened patiently; his gentle eyes fixed on hers as he comprehended the turmoil within her.

The wise elder smiled warmly and beckoned Sofia to join him in his garden. There, they stood before a beautifully crafted, ornate balance scale. Elias picked up two large and small stones and placed them on either side of the scale.

"Life, my dear Sofia, is like this balance," Elias began. "Each stone represents a role, a responsibility, a commitment. Just as the larger stone carries more weight, certain roles may demand more of your time and energy. But notice that the smaller stone has its significance too."

He carefully adjusted the balance until both stones rested at equilibrium. "See, Sofia, it's not about having equal weight on both sides at all times. Instead, it's about finding the right distribution so your life remains steady, harmonious, and purposeful."

Sofia gazed at the balanced scale, a glimmer of understanding in her eyes. Elias continued, "Remember that every role you embrace, every responsibility you bear, contributes to the beautiful mosaic of your life. Embrace each stone with dedication, but also know when to seek support, delegate, and find moments of rest."

Sofia felt a newfound sense of clarity as she absorbed Elias's words. It was as if a burden had been lifted, replaced by the wisdom that true balance doesn't demand perfection in all things but rather a wise distribution of one's energies.

With Elias's guidance, Sofia gradually learned to navigate her roles gracefully and wisely. She embraced the ebb and flow of life's demands, seeking harmony rather than perfection. And just as Elias had demonstrated with the balance scale, she found that even the smallest stones carried their own significance, contributing to the intricate masterpiece of her life.

This story illustrates the concept of balance and the importance of wisely managing various responsibilities and roles in life. It echoes the sentiment of the introduction—finding harmony amid life's complexities and challenges.

Everyone needs Balance: I vividly remember my dear niece, Bernadette, when she was just a three-year-old child. She used to joyfully sing a simple yet profound line, "Balance, balance, everybody needs balance," during our family gatherings. We would all laugh and playfully repeat this line whenever we felt overwhelmed or stressed. Little did we know that twenty years later, we would find ourselves penning the words of this book, exploring the very concept she innocently sang about.

Achieving Balance Requires Relentless Training: As we embark upon this literary voyage, delving into the pages of "The Balance Beam," we are not solely invited to explore the intricate interplay of faith, relationships, self-discovery, and purpose but also to draw inspiration from Simone's journey—her victories, trials, and the unwavering spirit propelling her onward. Much like Simone's relentless training, we too can train ourselves to attain that delicate balance, enabling us to confront life's trials with fortitude and treasure its joys with gratitude.

Divine Role in our Journey towards Achieving Balance in our Lives: Guided by the words of the Psalmist, "Delight yourself also in the Lord, and He shall give you the desires of your heart" (Psalm 37:4), we are urged to seek God's presence and align our desires with His divine plan. In the spirit of Simone Biles Owens and St Augustine of Hippo, let us embark upon this journey—a journey that transcends gymnastics, delving deep into the essence of harmonious living in a world where chaos and beauty coexist. May "The Balance Beam" illuminate our path as we navigate life's labyrinthine twists and turns, reminding us that genuine balance is found when we synchronise our steps with God's purpose, and our hearts resonate with His divine harmony.

So, dear readers, let us step onto the balance beam of life, guided by faith, as we explore the intricate dance of harmony that unfolds in the pages ahead. In a world where the demands of modernity often challenge our equilibrium, we will uncover the wisdom and guidance needed to traverse life's challenges with grace and celebrate its blessings with humility. Through the lens of "The Balance Beam," may we learn to balance the art of living on this delicate stage we call life.

The next chapter, Chapter 2, titled "The Artistry of Creation," invites us to dive deeper into the essence of existence. Building on our foundational understanding, we embark on a journey of awe and exploration. In this chapter, we marvel at the intricate details of the world around us, much like admiring an artist's masterpiece. Creation itself reflects the limitless creativity and wisdom of the Divine. As we journey through the next chapter, let us open our hearts and minds to the artistry surrounding us. Let us recognise that every aspect of creation, from the smallest atom to the grandest galaxy, is a testament to God's handiwork.

Chapter 2

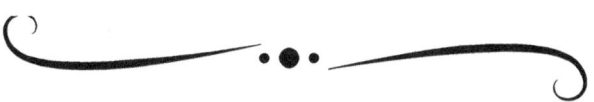

The Artistry of Creation

The symphony of creation resounds with the harmonious melody of God's artistry. From the vastness of the cosmos to the delicate intricacies of life, His design is woven with purpose, beauty, divine intention, and an incredible balance and harmony. As we journey through the canvas of creation, we discover the fingerprints of the Master Artist and unveil the profound truths that echo through the corridors of time.

Through the lenses of nature, science, and spirituality, we unravel the profound artistry woven into the fabric of reality, where everything harmoniously coexists. From the delicate intricacies of a flower's petal to the vast expanse of the cosmos, we encounter the diverse forms of beauty that grace our world. This exploration reveals how the natural world serves as a canvas for God's creativity, urging us to contemplate the mysteries and complexities that point directly to the Creator.

Nature is a Silent Bible: In the words of HH Late Pope Shenouda III, "Nature is a silent Bible, and the Bible is the speaking nature." As Pope Shenouda III beautifully articulated, creation is a testament to God's truth, revealing His majesty and wisdom. In every aspect of nature, we find reflections of His eternal word—a majestic symphony that speaks volumes without words. This silent symphony speaks to the hearts of those who listen to a profound narrative of God's presence and wisdom.

God's Creative Symphony: *For by Him all things were created that are in heaven and that are on earth, visible and invisible, whether thrones or dominions or principalities or powers. "All things were created through Him and for Him"* (Colossians 1:16). The overture of creation resonates with God's orchestration. Every celestial body, every mountain peak, and every whisper of wind bears witness to the Creator's handiwork; just as an orchestra follows a conductor in harmony, creation dances to the rhythm of God's divine baton.

Nature's Reverent Ode: *The heavens declare the glory of God; And the firmament shows His handiwork* (Psalm 19:1). Nature's tapestry is woven with threads of divine artistry. The canvas of the sky and the canvas of the heart reveal God's glory, inviting us to gaze upward and inward, recognising the Artist's signature in every stroke of creation.

The Poetry of Humanity: *"What is man that You are mindful of him, and the son of man that You visit him? For You have made him a little lower than the angels, and You have crowned him with glory and honor"* (Psalm 8:4-5). Humanity stands as poetry etched upon creation's pages. Created a little lower than the angels, we reflect God's glory in a unique way. The brushstrokes of our existence reveal the intention of the Master Artist—a portrait of divine dignity.

Custodians of Creation: *"Then God blessed them, and God said to them, 'Be fruitful and multiply; fill the earth and*

The Artistry of Creation

subdue it; have dominion over the fish of the sea, over the birds of the air, and over every living thing that moves on the earth'" (Genesis 1:28). Pope Francis embraced the stewardship notion, calling upon Christians to become "custodians of creation," and warning us to "safeguard creation, because if we destroy Creation, Creation will destroy us! Never forget this!" Delivering the message during his general audience in St. Peter's Square before more than 50,000 people, he adds, "Custody of creation is custody of God's gift to us, and a way of saying thank you to God. I am the master of creation, but to carry it forward, I will never destroy your gift." God entrusted humanity with the stewardship of creation. Like caretakers of a grand museum, we are called to honour, protect, and cherish the exquisite artwork of the natural world—a responsibility that echoes across generations.

Creation as a Living Testament: "The world is a great book, of which they that never stir from home read only a page," St. Augustine of Hippo. Saint Augustine reminds us that creation is a living testament to God's wisdom. To truly appreciate its beauty and significance, we must venture beyond our comfort zones and explore the pages of this majestic book. The canvas of creation unfurls as a testimony to the Master Artist's ingenuity. With every sunrise, with every dawn, every mountain's peak, and every gentle rustling leaf, creation declares the glory of its Creator. As we delve into the artistry of creation, we discover not just the majesty of nature but also the profound truths that underlie our existence. In the intricate strokes of God's design, we find an invitation to reflect His glory, steward His creation, and join the symphony of divine harmony reverberating through all creation.

In essence, a young Christian family can discover profound insights into God's meticulous craftsmanship and the harmonious equilibrium woven into creation by simply observing the world around them. Despite the universe's intricate and sometimes puzzling nature, an inherent equilibrium maintains its order. Similarly, amid the hustle and demands of life, young families can find value in pausing to assess their surroundings. Delving into the world's beauty and recognising the divine trust placed upon them encourages the pursuit of balance, even in the face of challenges—progressing one step at a time.

Having marvelled at the intricate artistry of creation, we now shift our focus to the pinnacle of God's creative expression: humanity. In Chapter 3, "Humanity's Unique Role," we explore our sacred place in the tapestry of existence as active participants, not mere observers, with lives infused by God's intention. Through Scripture and reflection, we uncover our purpose and responsibilities. This role involves stewardship, care, and fellowship, shaping the symphony of life with our actions. This exploration deepens our purpose and understanding and urges us to engage in God's ongoing masterpiece.

Chapter 3

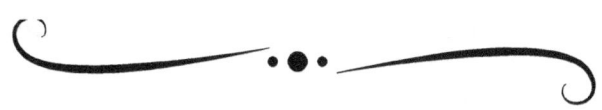

Humanity's Unique Role

In the grand tapestry of creation, humanity stands as the masterpiece—the crown of God's creative genius. Endowed with purpose, potential, and the divine image, each individual is woven into the intricate design of life. As we explore humanity's unique role, we unravel the threads of purpose, stewardship, and the sacred responsibility bestowed upon us.

Crafted in God's Image: Unveiling the Masterpiece Within

In the timeless tapestry of existence, the pinnacle of God's creative artistry emerges in the form of humanity. From the dawn of time, the divine hands of our Creator meticulously fashioned us in His image, an exquisite masterpiece that reflects His essence, wisdom, and love. As we explore this profound truth, we embark on a journey to understand the depth of our identity, purpose, and the remarkable significance of being crafted in the image of God.

The Divine Imprint: *"So God created man in His own image; in the image of God He created him; male and female He created them"* (Genesis 1:27).

This foundational truth resonates through the ages. Humanity stands as a living testament to the Creator's design. With intentional artistry, He sculpted each of us in His image, endowing us with the faculties to reason, create, and love. Every aspect of our being reflects a facet of God's nature, unveiling His divine fingerprint imprinted within us.

A Reflection of Relationship: *"Behold what manner of love the Father has bestowed on us, that we should be called children of God!"* (1 John 3:1).

In our image-bearing identity, we discover the profound reality of our relationship with God. Just as children resemble their parents, we carry the likeness of our Heavenly Father. This connection goes beyond physical resemblance; it extends to the spiritual realm—a truth that fills our hearts with awe and wonder.

Stewards of Creation: *"Then God blessed them, and God said to them, 'Be fruitful and multiply; fill the earth and subdue it; have dominion over the fish of the sea, over the birds of the air, and over every living thing that moves on the earth'"* (Genesis 1:28).

Crafted in God's image, humanity was entrusted with the stewardship of creation. We are called to care for the earth, mirroring God's role as the Creator and Sustainer of all things. Our responsibility extends to cultivating the world around us, reflecting the divine attributes of care, love, and order.

Humanity's Unique Role

The fall and Redemption: *"For as in Adam all die, even so in Christ, all shall be made alive"* (1 Corinthians 15:22).

While created in God's image, humanity bears the weight of sin, a shadow that mars the perfection of our reflection. The fall shattered the fullness of our image-bearing capacity, yet the divine image is restored through Christ. Our journey with Christ brings transformation and renewal, allowing us to reflect God's image more clearly.

Living Mirrors: *"But we all, with unveiled face, beholding as in a mirror the glory of the Lord, are being transformed into the same image from glory to glory, just as by the Spirit of the Lord"* (2 Corinthians 3:18).

As living mirrors of God's image, we are offered the privilege of being transformed by the Holy Spirit through baptism. Through our relationship with our Lord and Saviour Jesus Christ, we are continually shaped, renewed and refined through the sacrament of repentance and confession, and the role of His edifying words becoming more like Him in character and purpose. Our lives become a testament to God's ongoing masterpiece, His work of artistry within us.

A Call to reflect: *"Let your light so shine before men, that they may see your good works and glorify your Father in heaven"* (Matthew 5:16).

Crafted in God's image, we are called to illuminate the world with His radiant divine attributes. Our actions, attitudes, the sweet aroma of Christ and love should reflect the character of our Creator. Through our lives, we become a living testimony to the reality that we are fashioned in His image.

In the intricate threads of our existence, we discover the breathtaking reality of being crafted in God's image. This truth shapes our identity, purpose, and how we relate to God, creation, and one another. As we embrace our role as divine reflections, we enter into a deeper understanding of our place in the grand narrative of creation—an image-bearer called to radiate God's love, truth, and beauty in a world that longs for the light of its Creator.

Crafted in God's Image: *"Then God said, 'Let Us make man in Our image, according to Our likeness...'"* (Genesis 1:26).

The Creator's divine brush adorned humanity with His image, a mark that sets us apart in creation. Each person is a living canvas reflecting God's character, creativity, and capacity for love.

Immersed in Purpose: *"For we are His workmanship, created in Christ Jesus for good works, which God prepared beforehand that we should walk in them"* (Ephesians 2:10).

With purpose woven into our very being, we're called to embrace our unique roles with intention. Just as each gymnast brings their grace to the balance beam, every individual contributes a unique hue to the mosaic of humanity's story.

Unity in Diversity: *"For as the body is one and has many members, but all the members of that one body, being many, are one body, so also is Christ"* (1 Corinthians 12:12).

In our diverse roles, we find unity within the body of Christ. Just as a gymnastics team harmoniously works together, humanity flourishes when we celebrate and honour the unique contributions of each individual.

Nurturing Relationships: *"Husbands, love your wives, just as Christ also loved the church and gave Himself for her"* (Ephesians 5:25).

Within the tapestry of human relationships, marriage exemplifies selfless agape (love), sacrifice, and partnership. Like the graceful cooperation between gymnasts, couples are called to honour, uplift, and support each other on life's balance beam.

In humanity's unique role, we witness the divine artistry. Like a masterpiece on the balance beam, each individual has a

Humanity's Unique Role

role to play—a purpose to fulfil. As we explore this dimension of existence, we delve into the heart of God's creative intent and discover that each of us is fearfully and wonderfully made.

Just as Simone Biles Owens executes her routines with precision, humanity is called to fulfil its role with dedication and purpose. Each step, each choice, and each relationship are an integral part of the greater design. Let us embrace our role with gratitude, knowing that we are woven into a larger narrative that reflects the Creator's heart and culminates in a tapestry of divine harmony.

As we conclude our contemplation of humanity's unique role in the grand tapestry of creation, we now turn our gaze upward, beyond ourselves, and into the heavens. Just as we are endowed with purpose and responsibility, so too is the celestial realm governed by divine order and purpose. This sets the stage for our next chapter, where we will explore the captivating interplay between light and darkness, day and night.

In Chapter 4, "The Dance of Day and Night," we will delve into the exquisite choreography that unfolds in the heavens above. The sun's radiant ascent and gentle descent and the moon's luminous embrace of the night sky are not mere phenomena but a sublime display of God's artistic brilliance. Through the rhythmic dance of day and night, we witness the punctuated rhythm of creation, an intricate pattern that serves as a reminder of the Creator's unfailing constancy.

Drawing inspiration from the celestial ballet, we will reflect on the significance of light and darkness in the physical world and the tapestry of our lives. Just as day and night bring their unique blessings and challenges, we also navigate the seasons of clarity and obscurity, growth, and rest. The sun's warmth and light offer sustenance and visibility, while night's gentle hush provides a canvas for dreams and contemplation.

The Balance Beam

As we embark on this coming chapter, let us ponder the profound symbolism embedded in the day and night dance. It mirrors the ebb and flow of life's rhythms, reminding us that as night inevitably gives way to dawn, our moments of darkness yield to the light of hope and renewal. Together, let us explore the celestial spectacle that continues to unfold above us and within us as we contemplate the dance of day and night in the eternal choreography of creation.

Chapter 4

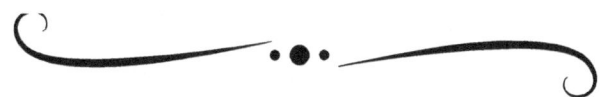

The Dance of Day and Night

Amid the celestial expanse, a mesmerising dance unfolds, the graceful waltz of day and night. With each turn of the earth, the sun and the moon harmoniously take their turns upon the cosmic stage. This eternal choreography, scripted by the Creator's hand, reveals profound truths illuminating human existence's ebb and flow.

Divine Rhythm: *"And God said, 'Let there be lights in the firmament of the heavens to divide the day from the night; and let them be for signs and seasons, and for days and years...'"* (Genesis 1:14).

The heavens became storytellers, weaving a narrative of purpose into the fabric of time. The sun and the moon became celestial timekeepers, guiding humanity through the rhythm of days and seasons. In their cadence, we glimpse God's meticulous design.

Dawn's Prelude: *"The night is far spent; the day is at hand. Therefore let us cast off the works of darkness, and let us put on the armor of light"* (Romans 13:12).

As dawn rouses the world from slumber, it becomes a metaphor for spiritual awakening. The light dispels darkness, urging us to cast off the shadows of sin and clothe ourselves in the armour of righteousness, aligning our lives with the Creator's purpose.

The Twilight of Reflection: *"The heavens declare the glory of God; And the firmament shows His handiwork. Day unto day utters speech, and night unto night reveals knowledge"* (Psalm 19:1-2).

The tapestry of day and night becomes a silent sermon. Just as the night unveils the splendour of stars, we are reminded of the Creator's boundless wisdom. The cycle of reflection during the night teaches us to meditate on His divine truths.

Hope in the Morning: *"Weeping may endure for a night, but joy comes in the morning"* (Psalm 30:5).

The night may shroud the world in darkness, but it is often a prelude to the dawn of hope. Just as the night gives way to the morning sun, our trials can yield to the promise of joy that God's mercy brings.

The Sovereignty of the Creator: In his remarkable words of wisdom, Saint John Chrysostom teaches us: *"Even if the devil throws trials upon you as thick as hail, or assails you with temptations and tribulations, and afflicts you with a multitude of ills, yet does he nothing beyond his power; for he is not the creator of the world, but a servant."*

Saint John Chrysostom's insight underscores the sovereignty of the Creator over the dance of day and night. Amid life's challenges and triumphs, God remains the Master Omnipotent, Omniscient, Omnipresent and Omnibenevolent, orchestrating every step of the cosmic ballet.

Unchanging Faithfulness of the Creator: In the ceaseless ballet of day and night, we witness the cosmic rhythm of God's creation. The unfolding drama of dawn, the quiet introspection of night, and the promise of morning joy mirror the cadence of our own lives. As the sun and moon perform their celestial choreography, they remind us that God orchestrates a harmonious symphony even in the dance of contrasts. Just as the night yields to the day and the day to the night, may we find solace in the unchanging faithfulness of our Creator, who guides us through life's seasons with His eternal grace.

In the poetic interplay of day and night, we glean profound lessons that resonate deeply with the journey of young families. The celestial ballet mirrors the cadence of our own lives, offering insights that can guide and inspire us in our pursuit of a God-centred and harmonious family life.

Embracing Life's Rhythms: Just as the sun and moon gracefully transition between day and night, young families can learn to embrace the ebb and flow of life's seasons. There are moments of brightness and joy, as well as periods of introspection and rest. By recognising that each phase serves a purpose in the grand narrative of our lives, families can navigate challenges with patience and hope, knowing that God's hand is guiding them through every transition.

Finding Balance in Contrasts: The cosmic ballet of day and night embodies the dance of contrasts. In the same way, young families can learn to navigate the contrasting demands and responsibilities they face. Balancing work and family time, finding moments for self-care amidst busyness, and cultivating spiritual growth amid daily routines require a delicate harmony, much like the celestial dance of light and darkness.

Embracing God's Faithfulness: The unchanging pattern of day turning to night and night yielding to day reflects God's unwavering faithfulness. Just as the sun rises without fail, God's grace and presence are constants in our lives. Young families can draw comfort from this assurance, knowing that no matter their challenges, God's love and guidance remain steadfast, guiding them through life's uncertainties.

Trusting God's Timing: The cosmic rhythm of day and night reminds us of the beauty of timing. Similarly, young families can learn to trust God's perfect timing for every aspect of their lives. Whether waiting for blessings, making decisions, or navigating transitions, placing their trust in God's timing can alleviate anxiety and foster a sense of surrender to His divine plan.

Reflecting God's Design: Just as the sun and moon follow their appointed paths, young families can align their lives with God's design. Just as the night complements the day and vice versa, each family member plays a unique role in the family's tapestry. Recognising and celebrating these roles fosters unity and harmony, mirroring the intricate choreography of creation.

Drawing Strength from Nature: The ceaseless ballet of day and night unfolds in nature's backdrop, inviting young families to draw inspiration from the world around them. Spending time outdoors, observing nature's cycles, and marvelling at its beauty can serve as a reminder of God's artistry and His role as the Master Choreographer of our lives.

In the cosmic rhythm of day and night, young families find a symphony of wisdom and insight. From embracing life's changing rhythms to finding balance in contrasts, from trusting God's unwavering faithfulness to aligning with His design, the celestial dance becomes a metaphor that guides families on their journey. Just as the sun and moon continue their cosmic ballet, young families can continue their own dance through life, guided by their Creator's unchanging grace and love.

As we conclude our reflection on the dance of day and night, we transition from contemplating the rhythms of creation

The Dance of Day and Night

to exploring our role within it. The beauty and order we find in the celestial ballet are a testament to God's meticulous design and faithfulness in upholding the universe. This serves as a backdrop for the next chapter of our journey, where we delve into the principles of stewardship and responsibility.

Just as the sun faithfully rises and sets, we are also called to steward the resources and responsibilities God has entrusted us faithfully. The rhythm of creation teaches us that all things have a purpose and a season, and it's our responsibility to maintain this delicate balance. We are called to be wise stewards, using our gifts, talents, and resources to nurture and preserve the world around us.

In the next chapter, we explore the concept of stewardship as a reflection of our gratitude to God. We will delve into how our actions, individually and collectively, can profoundly impact the world we inhabit. From caring for the environment to using our talents to serve others, our role as stewards is woven into the fabric of our faith.

Drawing inspiration from the dance of day and night, we will reflect on the rhythmic ebb and flow of life's seasons and how they mirror the cyclical nature of stewardship. Just as the world experiences times of growth and rest, so do our efforts to care for God's creation require both active engagement and moments of renewal.

Chapter 5

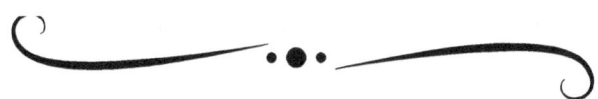

Stewardship and Responsibility

In the grand theatre of creation, humanity assumes the role of steward, a caretaker entrusted with the intricate balance of the natural world. With this stewardship comes an immense responsibility to nurture, protect, and preserve the beauty woven into the tapestry of life. As we delve into the concept of stewardship, we uncover the echoes of divine purpose and the call to safeguard God's masterpiece.

As we embark on this chapter, let us be mindful of the interconnectedness of all things and the privilege we have been given to participate in God's ongoing work of creation. Through our actions, we can contribute to His creation's flourishing or its degradation. With the day and night lessons as our guide, let us embrace the call to responsible stewardship, recognising that our faithfulness echoes the faithfulness of the One who orchestrates the cosmic dance.

Custodians of Creation: *"Then God blessed them, and God said to them, 'Be fruitful and multiply; fill the earth and subdue it; have dominion over the fish of the sea, over the birds of the air, and over every living thing that moves on the earth'"* (Genesis 1:28).

God's charge to humanity as stewards resounds through time. Our dominion is not one of exploitation but one of responsible care. Just as a caretaker tends to a garden, we are entrusted with the delicate balance of ecosystems. Our role is not to dominate but to collaborate harmoniously with the natural world.

Harmony with Creation: *"The righteous man cares for the needs of his animal, but the kindest acts of the wicked are cruel"* (Proverbs 12:10).

Stewardship extends beyond human interests; it encompasses compassion for all creatures. This verse echoes a call to exhibit kindness and empathy towards the animals under our care. As stewards, we are called to mirror God's kindness by nurturing and caring for the animals and ecosystems that share this planet.

Guardians of Tomorrow: *"For we know that the whole creation groans and labors with birth pangs together until now"* (Romans 8:22).

Creation itself anticipates restoration to gain redemption from the consequences of human mismanagement. As stewards, we are responsible for tending to creation's wounds, participating in its renewal, and protecting it for future generations. This verse from Romans highlights creation's interconnectedness and yearning for renewal, emphasising the urgency of responsible stewardship. *"The earth and the fullness thereof are a gift of God to men. We are trustees and stewards of God's property"* Clement of Alexandria.

Clement of Alexandria's words illuminate the concept of stewardship as a divine trust. Our role as stewards is not one

Stewardship and Responsibility

of ownership but of trusteeship. We are entrusted with God's creation, and our actions should reflect our understanding of its sacredness.

Divine Collaboration: *"Then the Lord God took the man and put him in the garden of Eden to tend and keep it"* (Genesis 2:15).

Adam's role as the first steward in the Garden of Eden exemplifies the partnership between humanity and God. Stewardship is not a solitary endeavour. It is a collaboration with the Creator in the ongoing preservation of His creation. This verse underscores that our role as stewards is embedded in the very fabric of our existence.

Stewardship is a sacred responsibility, a calling to be attentive custodians of the world around us. Just as God entrusted us with dominion, He also expects us to wield it with wisdom and care. The echoes of divine purpose resound as we recognise that stewardship is not a mere task but a reflection of our relationship with the Creator. Through our stewardship, we honour God's artistry, embody His kindness, and contribute to the healing and flourishing of the world. As we acknowledge our role as stewards, may we tread the path of responsibility with reverence and humility, understanding that the legacy of our stewardship shapes the legacy we leave behind for future generations.

Embracing Diversity: As we conclude our exploration of the principles of stewardship and responsibility, we find ourselves standing at the threshold of another vital aspect of Christian living: the embrace of diversity. Just as we've learned the importance of stewarding God's gifts and resources, we are now called to steward the diverse tapestry of humanity He crafted. Our journey from responsible stewardship to embracing diversity is a seamless transition, for in both cases, we are entrusted with the care and enrichment of God's creation.

In the same way that we've recognised our role as caretakers of the earth and all that dwells within it, we must now extend our sense of responsibility to include the diverse cultures, backgrounds, and perspectives that enrich our global community. The call to stewardship isn't limited to tangible resources; it extends to the intangible but equally precious aspects of God's creation: the people who bear His image.

Embracing diversity isn't just a societal virtue; it's a spiritual Christian imperative deeply rooted in our faith. Throughout Scripture, we find examples of God's delight in the rich tapestry of humanity. From the Tower of Babel to the day of Pentecost, God's handiwork in creating diverse languages, cultures, and nations is evident. This diversity reflects His infinite creativity and is a testament to His desire for a world where unity is forged through understanding, respect, and love for one another.

As co-creators with God in the stewardship of His magnificent creation, we come to value the intricate equilibrium that the Creator has woven into the fabric of existence. It is a profound privilege and a weighty responsibility bestowed upon humanity to comprehend and preserve this delicate equilibrium. This concept resonates strongly with the image of a Balance Beam. Much like the broader ecosystem, our lives require a harmonious interplay of various elements. For Christian families, both young and seasoned, grasping and upholding this balance is of paramount importance. It necessitates a deliberate pursuit, a conscious effort to tread this fine line. While undoubtedly challenging, we find invaluable guidance in the very act of creation.

Practising kindness towards all living beings in our sphere cultivates compassion in our hearts and paves the way towards achieving the equilibrium we seek. This extends not only to our interactions with the world around us but also to how we treat ourselves. By being attuned to the needs and well-being of others, we inherently cultivate a sense of self-compassion and nurture a healthier balance within our own lives.

In the next chapter, we delve into the significance of embracing diversity within the context of Christian living. We will explore the lessons nature and Scripture offer us, reminding us that God's design includes a vibrant mosaic of differences. Just as the Body of Christ is composed of many parts, each with its unique function, so is the world composed of many cultures, each contributing to the beauty and complexity of the whole.

Chapter 6

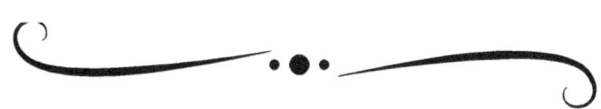

Embracing Diversity

In the magnificent mosaic of creation, diversity emerges as a hallmark of God's artistic brilliance. From the varied landscapes to the kaleidoscope of cultures and peoples, diversity enriches the tapestry of life. In embracing diversity, we acknowledge the richness of interacting with people with different perspectives, traditions, and stories. It's an opportunity to grow, to challenge our preconceptions, and to experience the transformative power of Christ's love as it bridges the gaps that divide us. By embracing diversity, we unearth the beauty of unity in multiplicity—a reflection of God's grand design.

In a world where divisions and misunderstandings often reign, embracing diversity becomes a powerful testament to our faith. It's a declaration that the love of Christ knows no borders and encompasses all people, regardless of their background. As we navigate this exploration, may we be inspired to understand the importance of embracing diversity and actively cultivating a spirit of unity, respect, and appreciation for the vast spectrum of humanity that God has created.

God's Diverse Palette: *"And He has made from one blood every nation of men to dwell on all the face of the earth..."* (Acts 17:26).

In the breathtaking scope of diversity, we discern the Creator's masterstroke. Every hue, culture, and ethnicity emanate from a common origin, revealing our shared humanity under God's creative hand. This verse from Acts underscores the divine intention behind the diverse array of people and cultures.

Unity amid Diversity: *"There is neither Jew nor Greek, there is neither slave nor free, there is neither male nor female; for you are all one in Christ Jesus"* (Galatians 3:28).

The words of Saint Paul serve as a radiant beacon, guiding us toward the unity we discover within the love of Christ. In the embrace of this love, we cultivate a shared identity that stands stronger than any earthly differences. As Saint John Chrysostom imparted, "Let us be bound together by the bonds of love, imitating the unity of the Holy Trinity. Just as the Father, Son, and Holy Spirit are distinct yet inseparable, so too are we, His children."

In the embrace of Coptic Orthodoxy, we are beckoned to embody the unity celebrated in Saint Paul's words. Just as the mosaic pieces find their place to form a masterpiece, so do we, diverse and distinct, find our place in the mosaic of God's love. In Christ, we are united, transcending the barriers that fragment our world. As we journey forward, let the wisdom of our Coptic Orthodox fathers guide us, reminding us that in Christ's unity, we find our true identity—a harmonious symphony of faith, love, and shared purpose.

Coptic Orthodox Wisdom: As the teachings of our revered Coptic Orthodox fathers affirm, our faith's core is unity. Just as a mosaic is composed of various coloured stones to form a magnificent whole, so are we, as the Body of Christ, woven together in unity despite our diverse backgrounds.

Our beloved Saint Athanasius, a beacon of faith, highlighted the importance of unity. He stated, "Just as the branches of a vine are intertwined and draw life from the same source, we, as believers, are united in Christ, drawing our spiritual life from Him."

In the same vein, Saint Cyril of Alexandria, a pillar of theological wisdom, emphasised that in Christ, we transcend the barriers that the world imposes upon us. He said, "In the Eucharist, we partake of the one body and blood of Christ. This participation unites us, making us members of His mystical Body and fostering an unbreakable bond of love and unity."

Embracing Diversity in Unity: In the rich tapestry of Coptic Orthodoxy, we find a heritage that cherishes diversity while upholding unity. Our Church, comprised of people from diverse cultures and walks of life, is a testament to the truth that unity in Christ transcends all worldly boundaries. Just as the various notes in a symphony blend harmoniously, so do our lives harmonise in the symphony of faith.

Unity beyond earthly divisions: The beauty of Coptic Orthodoxy lies in its unifying thread. As the great Saint Shenouda the Archimandrite illuminated, "In Christ, there is no distinction between Jew or Greek, slave or free, male or female." All in Him are one—a spiritual kinship that supersedes all divisions, fostering love and fellowship among believers.

The Tapestry of Gifts: *"But now indeed there are many members, yet one body"* (1 Corinthians 12:20).

Just as a tapestry is composed of diverse threads, the Body of Christ is composed of diverse gifts and talents. Every member contributes a unique strand to the fabric of the Church, illustrating the beauty of collaboration amid diversity. This passage from 1 Corinthians emphasises the value of each individual's contribution within a united community.

The Spirit not a Race Matter: *"Christianity is an affair of the spirit, not of race, or nationality, or language, or custom"* - St. Jerome.

St. Jerome's insight reinforces the universality of Christianity, a faith that transcends cultural boundaries and embraces all who seek Christ. It reflects the truth that diversity is not an obstacle but a testament to the boundless reach of God's love. Jerome's perspective aligns with the early Church's emphasis on the inclusive nature of the Gospel.

Cultural Treasures: *"After these things I looked, and behold, a great multitude which no one could number, of all nations, tribes, peoples, and tongues, standing before the throne and before the Lamb..."* (Revelation 7:9).

The vision in Revelation paints a vivid picture of diversity gathered before God's throne. Our diversity is not diminished in the presence of God, it's celebrated, forming a beautiful symphony of worship. This vision offers a glimpse into the eternal reality where people from every corner of the earth unite in worship, embracing their unique identities while glorifying God.

Nurturing Empathy and Understanding: Embracing diversity fosters empathy and understanding. As young families encounter people from various walks of life, they develop the capacity to listen, learn, and appreciate different perspectives. This equips them to approach challenges and dreams with a broader and more compassionate outlook.

A Living Lesson for Children: Embracing diversity becomes a powerful lesson for children within the family. As they witness parents and caregivers honouring the dignity of every individual, they learn the value of respect, empathy, and love. These virtues, instilled at an early age, guide them to become compassionate and responsible members of society and provide a strong foundation and platform to nourish and practice a profound Christlike identity and mind without compromising our Christian, cultural and traditions.

Embracing diversity is an acknowledgment of God's creative artistry. Just as a skilled artist combines colours to craft a masterpiece, God weaves together diverse cultures, languages, and backgrounds to create a vibrant world. As we navigate the intricate threads of diversity, may we recognise that unity does not mean uniformity? Instead, it's a harmonious blending of unique voices and perspectives, reflecting the multifaceted nature of the Creator. In embracing diversity, we emulate Christ's love, which knows no bounds, and participate in a global chorus that glorifies the One who is the ultimate source of all diversity. Through our celebration of diversity, we affirm the inherent dignity of every individual and contribute to a world that reflects the beauty of God's creative genius. Embracing diversity is akin to acknowledging the intricate strokes of God's creative brush across the canvas of existence. Just as a master artist skilfully combines colours to craft a masterpiece, so does God intricately weave together humanity's diverse cultures, languages, and backgrounds to create a tapestry of vibrant and interconnected lives. It's a divine symphony of uniqueness that harmoniously blends to form the world as we know it.

In the Book of Revelation, Saint John's apocalyptic vision offers a glimpse into the heavenly realm, where diversity is not just celebrated but magnified in its splendour. In Revelation 7:9-10, he witnesses a multitude that no one could count, consisting of people from every nation, tribe, people, and language, standing before the throne and the Lamb, clothed in white robes, and holding palm branches. This imagery paints a vivid picture of the ultimate harmony that emerges from the diverse worship of God. Unity doesn't erase distinctions; rather, it transcends them, creating a harmonious mosaic that reflects the multifaceted nature of the Creator.

As we navigate the intricate threads of diversity in our earthly lives, we must understand that unity doesn't equate to uniformity. The unity we strive for isn't the suppression of differences but the celebration of them. Just as different musical notes come together to form a beautiful chord, various cultures, perspectives, and experiences blend to create a harmonious whole. It reflects the God who fashioned humanity with purposeful diversity, all of us bearing His image while reflecting His creativity.

By embracing diversity, we follow the example set by Christ, whose love transcends boundaries and knows no limits. His ministry demonstrated a profound care for individuals from all walks of life, irrespective of their cultural, social, or ethnic backgrounds. The parables He shared showcased the vastness of His Kingdom, where diversity is welcomed and celebrated.

Revelation 5:9-10 further reveals the centrality of diversity in God's redemptive plan. The imagery of a new song being sung to the Lamb underscores the idea that every voice, every language, and every background will contribute to the eternal chorus of praise. This global symphony is a testament to the beauty of God's creative genius, and our participation in it through embracing diversity is a way of joining in the eternal worship of our Creator.

Ultimately, in celebrating diversity, we honour the inherent dignity of every individual, recognising that each person is a unique creation bearing the imprint of God's artistry. Our journey of embracing diversity aligns us with God's purpose for His creation and contributes to a world that mirrors the harmony of the heavenly realm, where every voice matters, and every culture enriches the collective narrative. Just as God's diverse creation reflects His glory, our celebration of diversity magnifies His greatness and showcases His boundless love for all His children.

Embracing Diversity

Embracing diversity fundamentally entails recognising and appreciating the intrinsic worth each member of a diverse group brings to the collective. God's divine design celebrates our differences while uniting us in Him as one harmonious whole. Similarly, a Christian family comprises distinct individuals with distinctive qualities, requirements, and imperfections. Yet, they are all integral parts of the same body, which is Christ. Hence, it becomes imperative for every member of a Christian family to acknowledge these distinctions and comprehend that it is precisely through the diversity of roles that the family derives its strength and resilience.

As we transition to Chapter 7, we embark on an intriguing journey to glean wisdom from an unexpected source – the animal kingdom. Just as we've learned to appreciate the tapestry of cultures and backgrounds, we'll discover the profound insights nature's creatures can offer. Join us as we uncover the lessons animals teach us about life, unity, and the intricate interconnectedness of God's creation."

Chapter 7

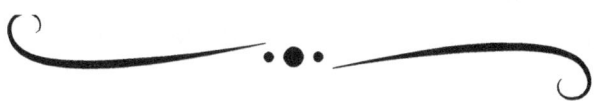

Lessons from the Animal Kingdom

Amid the wonder of creation, the animal kingdom emerges as a living parable, a source of wisdom and inspiration and profound balance and harmony. From the mightiest predators to the tiniest creatures, animals reveal profound lessons that resonate with the human experience. As we examine these lessons, we discover the Creator's intricate design and His intention for us to learn from His diverse creations.

Learning from the Ants: *"Go to the ant, you sluggard! Consider her ways and be wise, which, having no captain, overseer or ruler, provides her supplies in the summer, and gathers her food in the harvest"* (Proverbs 6:6-8).

The ant's diligence becomes a lesson in responsibility and preparedness. This verse encourages us to observe the wisdom embedded in nature and apply it to our lives to work with purpose and foresight.

Eagle's Renewal: *"But those who wait on the Lord shall renew their strength; they shall mount up with wings like eagles, they shall run and not be weary, they shall walk and not faint"* (Isaiah 40:31).

The soaring eagle becomes a symbol of spiritual renewal. Just as the eagle sheds its worn feathers for new plumage, those who wait upon the Lord find strength for their journey. This verse in Isaiah draws parallels between the eagle's physical renewal and the spiritual renewal of those who trust in God.

Early Church Father's Wisdom: *"Even the animals owe their life to God and ought not to be killed without his permission"* - Basil of Caesarea.

Basil of Caesarea's insight highlights the interconnectedness of all life forms and their dependence on God. This perspective invites us to respect and value the lives of animals, recognising them as part of God's creation.

Shepherd's Care: *"The Lord is my shepherd; I shall not want. He makes me to lie down in green pastures; He leads me beside the still waters"* (Psalm 23:1-2).

The imagery of the shepherd and his flock imparts a lesson in God's care. Just as a shepherd tends to his sheep, God guides and provides for His people. This Psalm reminds us of our dependence on the Good Shepherd's guidance.

Pope Shenouda III's Wisdom: *"The animals' joy is in their simplicity. When a person achieves simplicity, he attains the love of animals"* - Pope Shenouda III.

Pope Shenouda III's timeless wisdom resonates as a guiding light, illuminating the profound truth within animals' unassuming joy. Through these words, we glimpse the splendour of simplicity, the pure, unburdened essence that brings animals their innate happiness. This insight, drawn from the depths of Pope Shenouda III's spiritual wisdom, unveils a

Lessons from the Animal Kingdom

treasure trove of wisdom that holds transformative power for young families navigating the complexities of modern life.

In our modern world, where complexity often reigns and the cacophony of demands constantly reverberates, the pursuit of simplicity may seem like a distant aspiration. Yet, Pope Shenouda III invites us to contemplate the profound truth that simplicity is not a mere retreat from life's challenges but a portal to a deeper, more profound connection—with both the divine and the natural world around us.

Consider the animals, creatures whose existence is marked by an inherent harmony with their surroundings. Their joy emanates from an authentic state of being—uncomplicated, uncluttered, and unaffected by the artificial complexities humans often grapple with. In this simplicity, they find contentment devoid of striving, comparisons, or ego-driven pursuits. Pope Shenouda III's words remind us that this simplicity draws forth our admiration and love for the animal kingdom.

As we contemplate the essence of Pope Shenouda III's wisdom, we are guided towards the realisation that the embrace of simplicity holds the potential to rekindle our connection with God's creation and with our own spirituality. By shedding the layers of unnecessary complications that often cloud our vision, we create space for a profound communion with the divine. As animals find solace in their uncomplicated lives, so can we rediscover the joy of embracing a simpler way of being—one that aligns with our most authentic selves and God's design for our lives.

The wisdom encapsulated in Pope Shenouda III's insight extends an invitation to young families to cultivate simplicity in their lives. This is not a call to relinquish responsibilities or aspirations but an invitation to discern what truly matters. It beckons us to strip away the excess baggage that hinders our spiritual journey and embrace the beauty of the present moment, the depth of relationships, and the wonders of creation.

In a world of noise, distractions, and constant striving, the legacy of Pope Shenouda III's wisdom serves as a reminder that a life of simplicity is a life that radiates a unique charm. It resonates with the rhythms of creation and the essence of spirituality. By embracing simplicity, young families can create an environment where the love of animals—innocent, unpretentious, and free from ulterior motives—mirrors their own pursuit of a deeper, more meaningful connection with God, each other, and the world around them.

Spider's Tenacity: *"The spider skillfully grasps with its hands, and it is in kings' palaces"* (Proverbs 30:28).

The spider's determination to build its web even in challenging places becomes a metaphor for persistence and resourcefulness. This verse encourages us to learn from even the smallest creatures and their ability to adapt and overcome obstacles.

The animal kingdom serves as a classroom of divine wisdom, offering lessons that resonate with our human journey. From the ants' industriousness to the eagles' renewal, we find allegories that reflect God's truths. As we learn from the animal kingdom, we witness the Creator's intention for harmony and purpose in His creation. Let us embrace these lessons, humbly acknowledging that God's wisdom shines brightly even in the smallest creatures. Through our observation and reflection, we uncover treasures of insight that enrich our lives and deepen our connection to the Creator of all life.

In conclusion, as we contemplate the resilience of the animal kingdom and the grace of gymnasts on the Balance Beam, we find profound lessons that can enrich the lives of young Christian families. We are challenged to embrace resilience, discipline, and cooperation, striving to achieve a balance that sustains us and reflects the divine image in which we are created.

As we draw inspiration from the intricate lessons of the animal kingdom, we now transition into a profound exploration of 'Walking in Divine Balance.' Chapter 8 invites us to delve deeper into the art of harmonising our spiritual journey with the demands of our daily lives. Just as we've observed the delicate balance in nature's patterns, we'll uncover the wisdom of finding equilibrium in our faith, relationships, and responsibilities. Join us in embracing the transformative journey of aligning our souls with God's divine harmony, even amid the complexities of our human existence."

Chapter 8

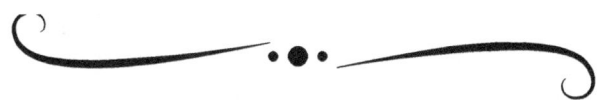

Walking in Divine Balance

As we conclude our exploration of maintaining the delicate balance of life, we find ourselves standing at the crossroads of faith and daily existence. The journey we have undertaken, guided by the wisdom of Scripture, early Church fathers, and the lessons of creation, brings us to a pivotal moment of reflection and commitment.

Divine Harmony: *"And we know that all things work together for good to those who love God, to those who are the called according to His purpose"* (Romans 8:28).

In the tapestry of life, God masterfully weaves every thread, every experience, and every moment into a harmonious symphony of purpose. This verse from Romans serves as a reassuring melody that resonates throughout our lives. It reminds us that, like a skilled conductor, God orchestrates every note, every twist, every rise and fall of our existence, all culminating in a grand composition that is uniquely our own.

Just as an artist blends colours on a canvas to create a masterpiece, God seamlessly intertwines our successes, failures, joys, and sorrows to craft a narrative that unfolds with purpose and meaning. This divine arrangement might not always be immediately evident; sometimes, life's events may appear disparate, like scattered musical notes. Yet, in the grand performance of our lives, God transforms these seemingly disconnected moments into a symphony of grace.

Through the melody of this verse, we find solace in knowing that our journey is part of a divine plan guided by the hands of a loving Creator. Even amidst challenges that might appear discordant, God is weaving a beautiful tapestry of purpose, where each note contributes to the masterpiece, He envisions for us.

At times, we might face a dissonant chord, a hardship, a setback, a loss. In these moments, it's easy to lose sight of the harmonious whole that God is creating. However, just as a musical piece may contain moments of tension before resolving into a harmonious chord, our lives, too, experience tension that will eventually resolve into divine harmony.

So, as we navigate the complex movements of life's composition, let us remember that even when the melody seems unclear, God is conducting a masterpiece of purpose. As we move through the different rhythms and tempos, we are part of a divine symphony that resonates across time and eternity. Through every twist and turn, through every high and low note, let us embrace the truth that our lives are harmonised by the hands of the Ultimate Composer, who creates beauty from every note and orchestrates divine harmony in our journey.

Walking in Wholeness: *"But let patience have its perfect work, that you may be perfect and complete, lacking nothing"*

(James 1:4).

In the grand tapestry of life, the thread of patience weaves a crucial strand that contributes to our wholeness. This verse from James paints a portrait of patience as a refining force that leads us toward a state of completeness. Just as a sculptor moulds clay with patience and care, our journey toward wholeness requires us to navigate the ebb and flow of life's challenges and joys.

Patience, like a master craftsman, sculpts our character, moulding us into vessels of strength and resilience. The intricate process of becoming whole takes shape through the challenges we face, the setbacks we encounter, and the trials we endure. Each moment of patience is a step toward fulfilling our purpose and realising our potential.

Consider a puzzle—a seemingly disconnected collection of pieces that, when patiently assembled, form a complete and harmonious picture. Similarly, the pieces of our lives—our struggles, joys, lessons, and blessings—are brought together by the patient hand of time under the guidance of the Creator. Just as each puzzle piece contributes to the whole image, each experience, whether favourable or challenging, contributes to our journey of becoming whole.

In a world that often values speed and immediate gratification, embracing patience may seem counterintuitive. Yet, this verse teaches us that the process of patience, when allowed to work its perfect work, leads to a state of being "perfect and complete, lacking nothing." Patience refines our hearts, aligns our perspectives, and helps us find contentment in the present, trusting that each step is vital to our journey toward wholeness.

Through the lens of faith, we see that our Creator crafts moments of patience not as obstacles but as opportunities for growth. As we wait, endure, and persevere, we inch closer to the completeness God envisions for us. Patience is a teacher that nurtures our inner resilience, moulding us into the individuals we are meant to be.

Just as the potter takes time to shape clay into a vessel of beauty and purpose, God, our Divine Potter, shapes us through the artistry of patience. The trials we face, the struggles we overcome, and the moments of waiting all contribute to the masterpiece He envisions for our lives.

Therefore, let us walk in wholeness by embracing the patient journey that leads us to completeness. With each step we take, we become more refined, resilient, and aligned with the divine purpose for which we were created. Through the lens of patience, our lives take on new meaning as we recognise that every piece of our journey contributes to the grand mosaic of wholeness God intends for us.

Living in Contentment: *"Let your conduct be without covetousness; be content with such things as you have. For He Himself has said, 'I will never leave you nor forsake you'"* (Hebrews 13:5).

The pursuit of material gain often disrupts the balance of contentment. This verse from Hebrews reminds us that our ultimate satisfaction is found in God's presence—a truth that anchors us in times of plenty and times of want. We have devoted an entire chapter addressing this crucial virtue and weapon, facing the challenges of being overpowered by life's complexities.

Final Reflections: Our journey through the chapters of divine balance has revealed the Creator's artistry, the challenges we face, and the transformative power of living in alignment with God's purpose. Have you found your purpose? Just as creation's intricate harmony reflects the Creator's wisdom, our lives are a symphony that resonates with His divine plan.

In the footsteps of early Church fathers and guided by the light of Scripture, we stand at the threshold of living a life that embraces the divine equilibrium. Let our relationships, stewardship, values, and faith reflect the balance in God's perfect design. May our pursuit of balance be a testament to the One who orchestrates every facet of our lives. May our journey inspire others to discover the abundant life that awaits when we walk in divine harmony and balance.

As we conclude our exploration of the significance of maintaining divine balance in our lives, we shift our focus to the challenges that arise in the context of modern times. Chapter 9, 'Navigating Challenges in Modern Times,' delves into the unique complexities and trials that the present era presents to our faith and values. Join us as we examine how to preserve our spiritual equilibrium amidst the rapid changes, shifting norms, and digital age demands. Let's equip ourselves with insights and strategies to navigate these challenges while upholding our unwavering commitment to our Christian principles.

PART TWO

A CHALLENGING WORLD

Chapter 9

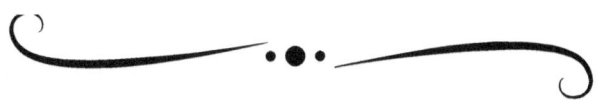

Navigating Challenges in Modern Times

In the ever-changing landscape of modernity, where advancements in technology, shifts in culture, and the complexities of life converge, the call to maintain balance resonates with particular urgency. As we navigate these challenges, we draw strength from the wisdom of Scripture, seeking guidance in preserving harmony in the face of the modern world's tumultuous currents. With a world that beckons us to be constantly connected, the tranquillity of balance becomes a refuge—a means to temper the rush and hum of modern life. The wisdom of Scripture resonates, guiding us to find equilibrium in the unceasing flow of change. In Proverbs 2:7, we read, *"He stores up sound wisdom for the upright; He is a shield to those who walk uprightly."* These words offer a haven, reminding us that amidst the whirlwind of transformation, we can find wisdom and protection in maintaining a balanced approach to life.

Overcoming Materialism: Transcending the Temptation of Materialism: *"Do not lay up for yourselves treasures on earth, where moth and rust destroy and where thieves break in and steal; but lay up for yourselves treasures in heaven, where neither moth nor rust destroys and where thieves do not break in and steal"* (Matthew 6:19-20).

In a world where the allure of material wealth and possessions often captivates our attention, the teachings of our Lord Jesus Christ emerge as a beacon of wisdom and discernment. His words resound like a clarion call, directing our focus toward an eternal perspective transcending earthly treasures' fleeting allure. As we navigate the labyrinth of material pursuits, these divine instructions provide a compass, guiding us through the treacherous waters of materialism and illuminating the path to true spiritual enrichment.

The verse from the Gospel of Matthew encapsulates a profound truth that resonates across the ages. Our Saviour's words invite us to pause and reflect on the impermanent nature of earthly riches—possessions susceptible to the ravages of time, decay, and theft. The metaphor of moth and rust evokes a vivid image of the transient nature of material goods, vulnerable to deterioration despite our best efforts to protect them. It is a poignant reminder that pursuing earthly treasures can often lead to disappointment and futility.

Yet, our Lord doesn't merely caution against material pursuits; He offers an alternative, a transformative paradigm shift that beckons us toward a higher purpose. He urges us to shift our focus from amassing temporal wealth to investing in treasures of eternal significance. These treasures, He assures us, are beyond the reach of moth and rust, beyond the clutches of thieves. They are treasures that flourish in the soul's realm and echo in heaven's eternal tapestry.

Navigating Challenges in Modern Times

In the cacophony of a world fixated on the accumulation of possessions, this divine guidance resounds with the promise of fulfilment that transcends the transient allure of materialism. The pursuit of heavenly treasures—the treasures of love, compassion, selflessness, and service—nourishes the spirit and fosters an enduring legacy that enriches both the giver and the receiver. These treasures are the investments that yield eternal dividends, echoing throughout eternity as a testament to a life well-lived.

As we strive to navigate the modern labyrinth of materialism, our Lord's teachings provide an unwavering anchor, reminding us of the ultimate purpose that transcends the temporal. His call to lay up treasures in heaven isn't merely a command; it's an invitation to embrace a life of profound significance that rejects the allure of the immediate for the promise of the eternal. Through this lens, we can navigate the complexities of material desires with discernment, wisdom, and a heart attuned to the treasures that truly matter.

May these words echo in the chambers of our hearts, prompting us to evaluate our pursuits, shift our priorities, and embrace the treasures that endure beyond time constraints. In a world that often clamours for more, may we find contentment in the wealth of a life lived in alignment with our Saviour's teachings—laying up treasures in heaven, where neither moth nor rust can tarnish and where the essence of our being finds its eternal home.

Our Lord's teaching invites us to adopt a perspective beyond immediate gratification, challenging us to consider the legacy we leave behind. By investing in heavenly treasures—acts of compassion, selflessness, and devotion—we cultivate a balance that transcends the allure of materialism. Our actions testify to our allegiance to a higher purpose, resonating with the eternal rhythm of God's kingdom.

Resisting Conformity: *"And do not be conformed to this world, but be transformed by the renewing of your mind, that you may prove what is that good and acceptable and perfect will of God"* (Romans 12:2).

The pressures of conformity tug at us, urging us to align with the world's values. Yet, the call to be transformed underscores the necessity of renewing our minds in God's truth and seeking His will, even amidst the currents of modernity.

Transforming Amidst Conformity: "And do not be conformed to this world, but be transformed by the renewing of your mind, that you may prove what is that good and acceptable and perfect will of God" (Romans 12:2).

Amidst the relentless pressures of conformity that seek to mould us according to the world's fleeting standards, the Apostle Paul's timeless exhortation to the Romans resonates as a clarion call for a transformation that transcends the bounds of societal norms. As we navigate the currents of modernity, this scripture serves as a guiding light, illuminating a path that leads us to a renewed mind—a mind steeped in the truth of God's Word and empowered to discern His perfect will.

The verse unfolds with a twofold imperative: resisting conformity and embracing transformation. In a world that often demands our allegiance to its ideologies, values, and trends, we are reminded not to allow ourselves to be shaped and moulded by its transitory allure—the prevailing currents of culture attempt to define our identity, priorities, and beliefs. Yet, we are beckoned to transcend the world's expectations, to stand firm as individuals who derive their identity from their Creator rather than conforming to the world's ever-shifting paradigms.

But resisting conformity is not enough; it is merely the first step. The verse directs our gaze toward the transformative power of renewing our minds. This transformation is not a superficial alteration of behaviour but a profound shift at the core of our being. It's a spiritual metamorphosis that unfolds through our continuous immersion in the truths of Scripture, the wisdom of God, and the guidance of the Holy Spirit. As our minds are renewed, we are empowered to discern what is good, acceptable, and perfect according to God's will—not the fleeting standards of the world.

The Apostle Paul's words echo across the ages, reminding us that transformation is not a passive process. It requires intentional effort and a deliberate turning away from the world's allurements. It calls us to cultivate a mind that is not swayed by every passing trend but one that is anchored in the unchanging truth of God's Word. This transformed mind becomes a beacon of light in a world dominated by shadows of conformity.

As we journey through the complexities of modernity, the call to resist conformity and embrace transformation is as relevant as ever. The pressures to conform are insidious, seeping into every facet of life—our values, beliefs, relationships, families, and aspirations. Yet, amid this cultural tide, the scripture points us toward a higher calling—a call to align our minds with the mind of Christ, to be agents of change rather than conformists of the mundane. What an amazing and honourable call!

Challenges: The transformative journey is not without challenges. It requires courage to swim against the currents of popular opinion, acceptance by others, comparisons with others and people's opinions to embrace values that may seem countercultural, and continually renew our minds in the truth of God's Word. Yet, the promise is both profound and liberating: through this transformation, we become conduits of God's will, vessels through which His good, acceptable, and perfect purpose is realised.

As we stand at the crossroads of conformity and transformation, may we heed the Apostle's call - do not be conformed to this world. May we refuse to be shaped by the world's mould and instead embrace the renewing work of the Holy Spirit. In a world that often seeks to define us, may we discover our true identity in Christ and radiate the transformative power of a renewed mind—one that not only resists conformity but also illuminates the path to God's perfect will amidst the complexities of modernity.

Maintaining Faith amid Doubt: *"For we walk by faith, not by sight"* (2 Corinthians 5:7).

The modern world often fosters doubt, demanding tangible proof for matters of faith. This verse from Corinthians reminds us that faith transcends the visible, urging us to find the balance between our spiritual convictions and the scepticism surrounding us.

In a world driven by empirical evidence and the demands for visible proof, the Apostle Paul's words to the Corinthians are a steadfast reminder of the tension between faith and doubt. Amidst the clamour of scepticism and the quest for concrete verification, this scripture invites us to find equilibrium. This delicate balance allows our faith to flourish even in the face of uncertainty.

The verse encapsulates a profound truth that resonates across the corridors of time. "For we walk by faith, not by sight." These words form a mantra for believers navigating the complexities of a modern world that often casts doubt on matters of faith. The dichotomy between faith and sight, the spiritual and the tangible, is a perennial challenge that requires discernment and a steadfast resolve to anchor our lives in the unshakable foundation of faith.

The modern age's emphasis on empirical evidence has led many to question the validity of beliefs that cannot be empirically proven. Doubt creeps in, whispering that faith is a relic of the past, incompatible with the rigour of rational thought. Yet, the scripture reminds us that faith is not synonymous with blind adherence. Instead, it's an intentional choice to trust in the unseen to embrace the spiritual dimensions that transcend the limitations of our senses.

Walking by faith does not imply a rejection of reason or surrendering to irrationality. Instead, it involves an acknowledgment that there are aspects of our existence that surpass the boundaries of human comprehension. Just as sight provides a limited perspective, faith invites us to explore the realms of the divine. This journey requires humility and an openness to mysteries that elude human explanation.

The tension between faith and doubt is not a sign of weakness but a mark of our humanity. Doubt itself can be a catalyst for growth—a prompting to seek more profound understanding and engage in earnest inquiry. Yet, the danger lies in allowing doubt to extinguish the flame of faith. The scripture offers a counterbalance, urging us to temper doubt with the unwavering conviction that there is more to reality than what meets the eye. Why did an Australian atheist philosopher move to Egypt to become a Coptic monk? Father Lazarus El Anthony is a Coptic monk living in seclusion in the Red Sea mountains in a 4th-century monastery about 200 miles southeast of Cairo, Egypt. A former university lecturer in literature and philosophy, Father Lazarus spent 40 years as an atheist. However, thanks to the doubt that worked as a catalyst for his amazing transformation, he adopted a new way of life.

Maintaining faith amid doubt requires a deliberate choice. It's an act of courage to embrace the intangible, to trust in a reality that transcends the material world. This choice is not blind but informed by the testimonies of those who have walked the path of faith before us and by the glimpses of the divine we encounter along our journey.

As we navigate the challenges of the modern world, the call to balance faith and doubt remains pertinent. The constant barrage of scepticism and the allure of visible proof may sway us, but the scripture calls us to stand firm. It encourages us to lean into faith—to walk the path guided by spiritual insight, even when empirical evidence may seem elusive.

The journey of faith is not a linear trajectory devoid of doubt; it's a dynamic dance between conviction and uncertainty. As we grapple with the tensions of our age, may we find solace in the scripture's wisdom. May we embrace the call to walk by faith, trusting in the unseen realities that anchor our souls. In a world that often challenges our beliefs, may we discover that true balance is found when faith and doubt coexist, each propelling us toward a deeper understanding of the mysteries of the divine.

Finding Rest in God: *"Come to Me, all you who labor and are heavy laden, and I will give you rest"* (Matthew 11:28).

The fast-paced modern life can lead to exhaustion and burnout. Jesus' invitation to find rest in Him offers solace and guidance as we navigate the demands of contemporary living.

A Balanced Spiritual Life: *"A spiritual life without balance becomes a life in the hands of chaos"* - Fr. Matta El-Meskeen.

Fr. Matta El-Meskeen's insight underscores the crucial nature of balance in our spiritual journey. Just as a ship needs balance to navigate stormy seas, our spiritual life requires equilibrium to navigate the challenges of modernity.

Amid the challenges posed by modernity, the call to maintain balance is not only relevant but imperative. Drawing on the enduring truths of Scripture and the insights of spiritual giants like Fr. Matta El-Meskeen, we navigate the complexities of materialism, conformity, doubt, and restlessness. As we uphold the divine equilibrium, we stand as beacons of light in the modern world—testimonies to the unwavering strength that comes from anchoring our lives in the timeless wisdom of God's Word.

In the rapidly evolving digital age, the chasm between those with access to technology and those without has become a significant societal challenge. This "digital divide" impacts education, communication, and opportunities, raising questions about the balance between technological advancements and social equality. As we examine this issue, we seek insights from both Scripture and contemporary perspectives to address the complexities of the digital divide.

Technology's Potential and Pitfalls: *"And whatever you do, do it heartily, as to the Lord and not to men"* (Colossians 3:23).

The digital realm offers incredible opportunities for communication, learning, and progress. However, this verse from Colossians reminds us that even in the digital sphere, our actions should be guided by a heart devoted to God, ensuring that technology is a tool for good rather than a source of division.

Justice and Equity: *"He who oppresses the poor reproaches his Maker, but he who honors Him has mercy on the needy"* (Proverbs 14:31).

The digital divide often deepens existing disparities, disproportionately affecting marginalised communities. This verse underscores the call for justice and compassion, inspiring us to bridge the gap and extend the benefits of technology to all, honouring God by aiding the less fortunate.

Embracing Responsibility: *"But take heed to yourselves, lest your hearts be weighed down with carousing, drunkenness, and cares of this life, and that Day come on you unexpectedly"* (Luke 21:34).

Technology's allure can distract from our spiritual focus and responsibilities. Just as Jesus warned against being weighed down by worldly concerns, we must be cautious not to allow technology to consume our time and attention to the detriment of our spiritual well-being.

Seeking Understanding: *"The heart of the prudent acquires knowledge, and the ear of the wise seeks knowledge"* (Proverbs 18:15).

Navigating the digital landscape requires wisdom and discernment. This verse encourages us to seek knowledge and understanding, enabling us to make informed decisions about technology's role in our lives and its potential impact on society.

The digital divide underscores the need to balance technological progress and social responsibility. By anchoring our approach to technology in Biblical principles, we can navigate the challenges of the digital age with wisely and rationally. As we strive for a world where technology unites rather than divides, let us remember that the call to love our neighbours extends to the digital realm, where justice, equity, and understanding must reign.

As we conclude our exploration of the challenges that modern times present to our faith and values, we turn our attention to a pervasive issue that many of us encounter: the busyness trap. In Chapter 10, 'The Busyness Trap,' we will dive into the fast-paced nature of our lives and how it can inadvertently lead us away from our core beliefs. Join us as we uncover the ins and outs of this phenomenon and discover strategies to navigate it while keeping our faith and well-being intact. Let's find a harmonious rhythm that allows us to thrive spiritually, mentally, and emotionally amid life's demands.

Chapter 10

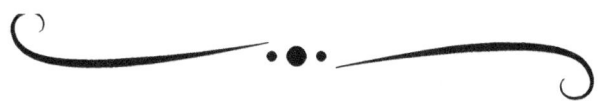

The Busyness Trap

In the modern era, the relentless pace of life often leads to a sense of perpetual busyness—a trap that can hinder our ability to find balance and meaning. The quest for success, coupled with the demands of daily life, can lead to burnout and a neglect of the essential aspects of our existence.

The essential aspects of our existence encompass various dimensions that contribute to a well-rounded and meaningful life. These aspects go beyond the material pursuits and encompass the deeper elements that nurture our overall well-being and sense of purpose. Embracing a Christ-centred Life:

As followers of Christ, our pursuit of balance should reflect the teachings of Jesus. He emphasised the importance of our spiritual well-being, urging us to seek first the Kingdom of God and His righteousness (Matthew 6:33). Our physical bodies, as temples of the Holy Spirit (1 Corinthians 6:19-20), should be cared for with gratitude and moderation. In our relationships, Christ's commandment to love one another guides us in fostering meaningful connections based on love, forgiveness, and compassion.

Growing in Christlikeness: As we grow in faith, we recognise that personal growth and learning involve aligning ourselves with Christ's character. We strive to renew our minds in Him (Romans 12:2) and continually conform to His image (2 Corinthians 3:18). This transformative journey includes embracing challenges and setbacks, much like the doubts that Thomas had and overcame through encountering the risen Christ (John 20:24-29).

Bearing Fruit in Service: Our faith prompts us to contribute to the well-being of others. We emulate Christ's example of selflessness through service and generosity. The Parable of the Good Samaritan (Luke 10:25-37) illustrates how our actions should reflect love for our neighbours as our Lord Christ commanded us.

Resting in God's Presence: Amid life's busyness, Christ offers us rest. He invites us to come to Him when weary and burdened, promising rest for our souls (Matthew 11:28-30). Times of rest and reflection allow us to draw closer to Him, seeking guidance and renewal.

Grateful Living: Being grateful is a foundational Christian virtue beyond mere words of thanks. It's a posture of the heart that acknowledges God as the ultimate source of all blessings. It's an attitude that recognises every good thing as a gift from a loving Creator, leading us to respond with a heart brimming with gratitude and praise.

The story of the ten lepers healed by Jesus, as recounted in Luke 17:11-19, beautifully exemplifies the transformative power of gratitude. In this narrative, ten individuals afflicted with leprosy approached Jesus, fervently pleading for

The Busyness Trap

healing. Touched by their faith, Jesus instructed them to show themselves to the priests. As they obeyed and began their journey, they were miraculously healed.

However, only one of the ten, a Samaritan man, turned back to Jesus, falling at His feet with a heart overflowing with gratitude. He praised God and thanked Jesus for the miraculous healing he had received. Jesus, moved by the Samaritan's genuine gratitude, commended him, and emphasised the significance of his response. He questioned the absence of the other nine and highlighted how this foreigner, who returned to give thanks, had experienced both physical and spiritual healing.

This story underscores several important aspects of grateful living:

1. **Recognition of Blessings:** Grateful living starts with recognising the blessings we receive. In the case of the lepers, healing from a debilitating disease was a profound blessing that transformed their lives. It's a reminder that even the most significant transformations in our lives deserve acknowledgment and thanksgiving.

2. **Returning to God:** The Samaritan's act of turning back to Jesus symbolises the importance of returning to God with a heart of gratitude. It signifies a realisation that God is the source of all blessings and that our response should be worship and thanksgiving.

3. **Complete Healing:** Beyond physical healing, the Samaritan also received spiritual healing. Jesus said, *"Your faith has made you well."* This reveals that gratitude and faith are interconnected. Expressing gratitude reflects faith and trust in God's goodness and provision.

4. **A Humble Heart:** Grateful living is an expression of humility, a recognition that we are recipients of God's grace and mercy. Falling at Jesus' feet demonstrates

the Samaritan's humility and acknowledgment of Jesus' divinity.

As Christians, grateful living is a way of life that aligns with our belief in a loving and benevolent Creator. It's a way of acknowledging God's hand in every aspect of our lives and responding with a heart of thanksgiving. Just as the Samaritan's gratitude brought him into a deeper relationship with Jesus, our gratitude draws us closer to God, cultivating a heart attuned to His blessings, grace, and unfailing love.

Incorporating these Christian principles into our pursuit of balance helps us live a life pleasing to God and aligned with His purpose. As we navigate the complexities of modern life, let us anchor our quest for balance in the unchanging truths of the Gospel and the example of Christ, finding fulfilment in His grace, love, and guidance.

Balancing these essential aspects of our existence allows us to lead fulfilling lives not solely defined by busyness and material success. When prioritising these dimensions, we create a more holistic and meaningful life that aligns with our values and contributes to our overall well-being. As we navigate the busyness trap, we turn to Scripture for guidance on how to live purposefully amidst the whirlwind of activities.

Priorities and Perspective: *"But seek first the kingdom of God and His righteousness, and all these things shall be added to you"* (Matthew 6:33).

The busyness trap often ensnares us when our priorities become disordered. Jesus' teachings remind us that the foundation of our pursuits should be the kingdom of God and His righteousness. This principle not only guides us in seeking divine purpose but also cultivates a mindset that thrives on eternal values rather than temporary gains.

Jesus' profound words in Matthew 6:33 echo through the corridors of time, urging us to reevaluate our pursuits and reorient our priorities. The bustling world around us constantly vies for our attention, tempting us to invest our time and energy in pursuits that can ultimately lead to exhaustion and spiritual emptiness. However, when we internalise the wisdom of these words, they become a beacon of clarity amid life's clamour.

This mindset takes root and grows within us—a conscious choice to put God's kingdom and righteousness at the forefront of our lives. It's an intentional decision to align our desires, plans, and actions with His divine will. As this mindset matures, we gradually break free from the trappings of busyness that threaten to distract us from what truly matters.

Furthermore, this principle isn't limited to our individual lives. As parents, imparting this foundational truth to our children is essential. Teaching them the value of prioritising God's kingdom and righteousness instils a compass that guides their decisions and actions. Just as Jesus emphasised simplicity and the eternal perspective, we have the privilege and responsibility to pass on these timeless principles to the next generation.

When we weave this mindset into our and our children's lives, we lay the groundwork for a future that thrives on purpose, balance, and lasting fulfilment. The busyness trap loses its grip as we teach our children the wisdom of seeking first God's kingdom, nurturing a legacy that values the eternal over the fleeting, the substantial over the superficial. As we align ourselves and our families with this divine truth, we uncover a pathway to a life of meaningful, God-centred abundance.

Rest for the Soul: *"Come to Me, all you who labor and are heavy laden, and I will give you rest"* (Matthew 11:28).

Amid busyness, Jesus offers rest for our weary souls. This verse invites us to find solace and rejuvenation in Him, recognising that true balance comes from surrendering our burdens to the One who provides true rest.

The Example of Mary and Martha: *"And Jesus answered and said to her, 'Martha, Martha, you are worried and troubled about many things. But one thing is needed, and Mary has chosen that good part, which will not be taken away from her.'"* (Luke 10:41-42).

The timeless story of Mary and Martha unfolds as a poignant reminder of the delicate balance between busyness and spiritual priorities. As Jesus entered their home, Martha found herself engrossed in preparations and tasks, while her sister Mary chose to sit at the feet of the Master, captivated by His presence and teachings. This scene encapsulates a universal struggle—caught between the demands of the world and the longing for meaningful communion with God.

Martha's earnestness and diligence were not without value. The tasks she busied herself with were legitimate responsibilities. Yet, in her flurry of activity, she missed a crucial aspect—the divine opportunity to bask in the presence of the Saviour. Jesus' gentle admonishment, "Martha, Martha, you are worried and troubled about many things," speaks to the pervasive tendency to allow busyness to eclipse the more profound matters of the heart.

In contrast, Mary's choice reflects a wisdom that transcends the external demands of the moment. Sitting at Jesus' feet, she embraced the "good part," recognising that the true treasure lay in nurturing her relationship with Him. This moment was not about neglecting responsibilities but about setting proper priorities—acknowledging that cultivating spiritual intimacy with God is the foundation upon which all other endeavours find meaning and purpose.

The lesson from this encounter echoes through generations. The bustling pace of life can easily lead us down Martha's path—filled with tasks, obligations, and distractions. The modern world often amplifies this struggle, bombarding us with incessant demands that vie for our attention. Yet, as

Jesus pointed out, "one thing is needed amidst the clamour." Amidst the ceaseless flurry of life's activities, the essence of our existence finds its centre in our relationship with God.

This story offers a transformative perspective on navigating the tension between busyness and spiritual priorities. It's not a call to abandon responsibilities or tasks but an invitation to approach them with a heart aligned with the "good part." When we prioritise time in God's presence, we infuse every task with purpose and meaning, recognising that His wisdom and grace ultimately guide our efforts.

As we reflect on the example of Mary and Martha, we're reminded that true balance emerges when our pursuit of God takes precedence over the world's distractions. Like Mary, may we choose the "good part," setting aside time to sit at the feet of our Saviour, allowing His presence to infuse every aspect of our lives. In this choice, we find the elusive harmony that transcends the busyness trap, allowing us to fulfil our responsibilities while nurturing the sacred bond that sustains our souls.

Contentment and Moderation: *"Now godliness with contentment is great gain"* (1 Timothy 6:6).

St. John Chrysostom emphasised that true contentment comes from our spiritual relationship with God rather than material possessions. He said: "Riches do not consist in the possession of treasures, but in the use made of them. These superfluous things are not true riches. They are most rich those who use the least. Let us not admire a rich man for his riches but for his life. It is not riches that make a person rich, but their use of them."

St. John Chrysostom's words underscore the importance of finding contentment not in accumulating worldly possessions but in how we live our lives and use what we have to bless others and draw closer to God. This perspective aligns with the biblical teaching that godliness with contentment is indeed a significant gain (1 Timothy 6:6).

In a world that constantly whispers the allure of more, contentment stands as a counter-cultural virtue—a steadfast reminder that true wealth is not measured by material accumulation but by the state of the heart. The verse from 1 Timothy 6:6 encapsulates this profound truth: "Now godliness with contentment is great gain."

The busyness trap often takes root in the pursuit of more—more possessions, more achievements, and more recognition. Yet, the unquenchable quest for "more" often leaves us perpetually dissatisfied, trapped in a cycle of never-ending striving. In contrast, the wisdom of this verse points us toward a different path that links godliness with contentment, revealing an invaluable treasure that far exceeds worldly gain.

Contentment doesn't imply complacency or a lack of ambition. Instead, it speaks to a heart posture that finds fulfilment in God's presence and provision. It's a state of mind that recognises the sufficiency of His grace and the richness of His blessings. As the apostle Paul wrote to the Philippians, "I have learned in whatever state I am, to be content" (Philippians 4:11, NKJV). This contentment isn't based on circumstances but on an unwavering trust in God's sovereignty and goodness.

Moderation, closely intertwined with contentment, guides us in managing our desires and ambitions. It's a principle that calls for temperance, balance, and self-control. Pursuing moderation safeguards us from the excesses that can lead to burnout, dissatisfaction, and spiritual emptiness. In a culture that often glorifies excess, the call to moderation reminds us that lasting satisfaction harmonises our desires with God's design.

The profound insight of this verse extends beyond personal well-being—it highlights the eternal perspective of godliness and contentment. A synergistic effect occurs when godliness—a life lived in reverence and devotion to God—is paired with contentment. Our pursuit of godliness shapes our values, ambitions, and priorities, leading us to recognise that true gain lies in aligning our hearts with His purposes.

Amid life's busyness, the call to cultivate godliness and contentment offers a lifeline of perspective. It redirects our focus from the fleeting to the eternal, from the noisy clamour of "more" to the serene satisfaction of God's presence. This verse beckons us to pause, reflect, and reevaluate the driving forces behind our pursuits.

As young families navigate the complexities of modern life, embracing contentment and moderation is a source of strength and stability. It's an invitation to set priorities prioritising spiritual growth, meaningful relationships, and an abiding connection with God. In choosing contentment over constant striving and moderation over excess, families discover a sustainable rhythm that counteracts the busyness trap, leading to a life marked by true gain. This life finds its treasure in the richness of God's love and the joy of His presence.

Pope Shenouda III's wisdom proposes: *"Do not allow busyness to prevent you from praying and evaluating yourself daily."* His insight directs our attention to the spiritual dimension of busyness. Amidst our tasks and responsibilities, we must prioritise moments of prayer and self-reflection to maintain a balanced and spiritually nourished life.

The busyness trap robs us of the precious moments that truly matter—our connection with God, relationships, and well-being. As we navigate this challenge, Scripture and the wisdom of Pope Shenouda III offer a blueprint for prioritising the eternal over the temporal, finding rest for our souls, and embracing a life of contentment and moderation. By learning from the lessons of Mary and Martha, we can strike a balance between our responsibilities and spiritual growth. Let us remember that true success lies not in the number of tasks accomplished but in the depth of our relationship with God and our ability to live intentionally in His presence.

In pursuing the demanding nature of the busyness trap and its potential to distract us from our core values, we're now poised to delve into another influential aspect of our lives: cultural influences. Just as the busyness trap can subtly shape our priorities, our cultural surroundings significantly shape our perspectives, beliefs, and behaviours. Chapter 11, 'Cultural Influences,' will guide us as we navigate the powerful currents of cultural norms, media, and societal pressures. Together, we'll uncover how to stay anchored in our Christian values while engaging thoughtfully with the world. Join us on this exploration of the interplay between faith and culture as we seek to forge a path that reflects the teachings of Christ in the midst of a dynamic and diverse society."

Chapter 11

Cultural Influences

The cultural milieu in which we live shapes our values, beliefs, and behaviours. While culture can enrich our lives, it also challenges maintaining a balanced Christian lifestyle. Navigating the currents of cultural influences requires discernment and a firm foundation in our traditions & Scripture. As we explore this dynamic, we seek wisdom to strike a harmonious balance between our faith and the world around us.

Remaining Unspotted: *"Pure and undefiled religion before God and the Father is this: to visit orphans and widows in their trouble, and to keep oneself unspotted from the world"* (James 1:27).

St. James highlights the need to remain unspotted by worldly influences. While engaging with culture, we are called to protect the purity of our faith and values. This verse underscores the balance between compassion for those in need and guarding our hearts from detrimental cultural elements.

Separation from the World: *"Do not love the world or the things in the world. If anyone loves the world, the love of the Father is not in him"* (1 John 2:15).

Cultural influences can entice us to prioritise worldly desires. John's admonition emphasises the need to maintain a healthy detachment from the world's allure, ensuring that our love for God remains undiluted by worldly affections.

Transformed Minds: *"And do not be conformed to this world, but be transformed by the renewing of your mind, that you may prove what is that good and acceptable and perfect will of God"* (Romans 12:2).

St Paul encourages us to resist conformity to worldly patterns. Instead, we are called to transform our minds through the renewal found in Christ. This verse guides us to seek a balance between cultural engagement and spiritual transformation.

Being Light in the Darkness: *"You are the light of the world... Let your light so shine before men, that they may see your good works and glorify your Father in heaven"* (Matthew 5:14,16).

Cultural influences provide opportunities to shine as lights in the darkness. Christ's words remind us that our actions and values should stand out, inspiring others to glorify God. Balancing cultural engagement with unwavering commitment to Christ can lead to impactful witness.

Wisdom from Abouna Bishoy Kamel: *"Our unity with God and His church should be stronger than our unity with the world."* - Abouna Bishoy Kamel

Abouna Bishoy Kamel's wisdom underscores the importance of prioritising our unity with God and the church over our alignment with worldly influences. This perspective guides our endeavour to balance cultural engagement with our Christian identity.

Cultural influences exert a powerful pull on our lives, shaping our worldviews and actions. As we navigate this complex terrain, we draw on the wisdom of Scripture and the insights of Abouna Bishoy Kamel to maintain a delicate balance. We honour God while engaging with the world by remaining unspotted, separating from worldly attachments, renewing our minds, and being intentional lights in darkness. Through discernment and a commitment to Christ, we find the equilibrium needed to live as faithful, transformative participants in our cultural context.

While navigating the powerful currents of cultural influences, we've delved deep into how they shape our perspectives, values, and choices. As we reflect on the impact of these influences, we recognise the delicate balance required to harmonise our faith with the practical aspects of daily life. This balance is at the heart of the upcoming chapter, where we explore how to bridge the gap between our unwavering faith and the pragmatic realities we encounter. Chapter 12: 'Balancing Faith and Practicality' will guide us through weaving spiritual principles into the fabric of our practical decisions, equipping us with insights to embrace a life where faith and practicality are not in conflict but rather work in harmony. Let's embark on this journey of discovering how to live authentically, grounded in our faith, while navigating the practical complexities of the world around us.

Chapter 12

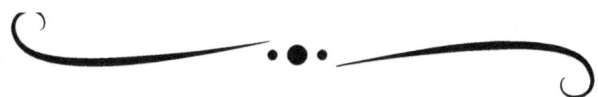

Balancing Faith and Practicality

The interplay between faith and practicality is a delicate dance that defines our Christian journey. While faith anchors us in spiritual truth, practicality guides us in navigating the complexities of everyday life. Striking a balance between these two aspects is crucial to living out our faith authentically. In this exploration, we draw insights from Scripture and three Christian stories—George Müller's faith-filled provision, the story of moving Al-Mokattam Mountain in Egypt harmonising the call to believe, and the call to live our beliefs practically.

Faith That Moves Mountains: *"So Jesus said to them, 'Because of your unbelief; for assuredly, I say to you, if you have faith as a mustard seed, you will say to this mountain, "Move from here to there," and it will move; and nothing will be impossible for you'"* (Matthew 17:20).

During a cherished pilgrimage to the holy city of Jerusalem, I found myself wandering along the narrow, time-worn streets that exude the authenticity of a place rich with history. Amid the city's bustling energy, my gaze was captivated by a simple yet intriguing sign adorning a sac nestled within an enchanting herbs shop. The sign bore the words "mustard seed."

Intrigued by this enigmatic phrase, I approached the shop owner with an eager smile and made my request known—I wished to purchase a mustard seed. I confessed that I had never laid eyes upon one before and was filled with curiosity about this seemingly unassuming seed that carried such significance.

The proprietor returned my smile with a warm one of his own and agreed to grant my request. With practised hands, he retrieved a sac resembling a walnut, cradling within it the precious mustard seeds. Anticipation heightened as he carefully opened the sac, revealing a cluster of seeds resembling those found in the depths of a blackberry.

Yet, the true revelation was yet to come. Taking one of the seeds, he skilfully cracked it open, unveiling a multitude of tiny, dark powder-like shapes. My amazement knew no bounds as he further crushed the seed, transforming it into an incredibly fine powder. I marvelled at the intricate details contained within this tiny seed—hundreds of minuscule, black powder fragments, each a testament to the intricate artistry of creation, and the man victoriously yet very kindly smiled and said, "here's your mustard seed!!"

The mustard seed took on a newfound significance at that moment, transcending its size and appearance. It became a tangible metaphor, a living parable of the extraordinary potential contained within the seemingly ordinary. This encounter was a gentle reminder that even the smallest of faith, when nurtured and cultivated, can yield a harvest of transformation and impact far exceeding its initial appearance.

Balancing Faith and Practicality

As I left the shop that day, mustard seed in hand, I carried with me a tangible souvenir and a profound lesson etched into my heart. Like our faith, the mustard seed starts small and unassuming, yet it holds within it the power to grow and flourish, enriching our lives and radiating God's divine purpose. As Christ Himself mentioned, "If you have faith as a mustard seed, you will say to this mountain, 'Move from here to there,' and it will move; and nothing will be impossible for you" (Matthew 17:20).

Jesus' words remind us of the power of even the tiniest seed of faith. Balancing faith and practicality doesn't mean forsaking the miraculous. Instead, it calls us to exercise unwavering faith while engaging in practical actions.

Moving Al-Mokattam Mountain: In the late 9th century, a Coptic Christian leader, St. Simon the Tanner, encountered the challenge of moving Al-Mokattam Mountain in Egypt. In the annals of Coptic history, an extraordinary event is a testament to the incredible power of faith, unwavering devotion, and the miraculous divine intervention. During the late 9th century, the revered Coptic Christian leader, St. Simon the Tanner, found himself facing an awe-inspiring challenge – the task of moving the seemingly immovable Al-Mokattam Mountain in Egypt. This incredible feat, achieved through a beautiful blend of faith, fasting, fervent prayers, and the resounding echoes of "Kyrie Eleison," became a shining example of the unyielding strength that faith can infuse into even the most insurmountable obstacles.

In the heart of Egypt, where the mountain cast its imposing shadow, St. Simon the Tanner was a beacon of faith and a shepherd to his fellow believers. The backdrop of his time was one of adversity, with the Coptic Christian community enduring persecution and seeking refuge from the challenges surrounding them. St. Simon's faith emerged as a radiant light in this crucible of trials, illuminating the path of hope for his people.

As the story goes, St. Simon, guided by his deep communion with God, embarked on an audacious endeavour – to move Al-Mokattam Mountain through the power of his faith. This daunting task wasn't simply a physical feat but a spiritual testament to the profound belief that God's omnipotence transcends the bounds of the natural world. St. Simon recognised that in order to achieve this extraordinary endeavour, he would need to draw upon the timeless spiritual practices that had fortified believers for generations.

Fasting, a practice rooted in spiritual discipline, became an integral part of St. Simon's preparations. Through fasting, he sought to purify his body and spirit, aligning himself more closely with God's will. St. Simon's connection with the divine deepened with each day of abstention, allowing him to tap into a wellspring of spiritual strength that transcended the physical realm.

Yet, the power of prayer truly set the stage for this miraculous event. Fervent supplications, heartfelt intercessions, and a ceaseless dialogue with the Creator marked St. Simon's days. With unwavering faith, he beseeched God's divine intervention, imploring for the mountain to be moved as a sign of His grace and a testament to the power of faith. The echo of "Kyrie Eleison," Lord have mercy, reverberated through the air, carrying the weight of an entire community's hopes and aspirations.

And so, the day of reckoning arrived – a day that would forever etch itself into the annals of history. With a heart full of faith and a spirit fortified by fasting and prayer, St. Simon stood before the mountain, ready to witness the impossible become possible. In response to his unwavering belief and the cries of "Kyrie Eleison," the mountain began to stir as if responding to the voice of God Himself. Slowly but surely, the massive earth mass began to shift, leaving an indelible mark

Balancing Faith and Practicality

on the physical landscape and the spiritual consciousness of those who bore witness.

St. Simon's incredible feat of moving Al-Mokattam Mountain stands as a timeless testament to the immense power of faith when coupled with disciplined spiritual practices. Through fasting, prayer, and unyielding trust in the divine, St. Simon harnessed a force that transcended the laws of nature, demonstrating human faith's potential to reshape the world around us. His story resonates through the ages, reminding us that when we anchor our actions in faith and align them with spiritual principles, even the mightiest mountains – whether literal or metaphorical – can be moved with the grace of God.

For young Christian families navigating the complex journey of life, the remarkable story of St. Simon's faith-driven triumph over the immovable Al-Mokattam Mountain offers not only a fascinating historical account but also a profound source of inspiration. While facing challenges and uncertainties in the modern world may differ from moving mountains, the principles underpinning St. Simon's extraordinary feat hold invaluable lessons for young families seeking solace, guidance, and strength in their own trials. How did he do it? A beautiful mix of a very unique recipe, faith, fasting, prayers, and lots of Kyrie Elision!

1. **Cultivating Unwavering Faith:** Just as St. Simon's faith was the cornerstone of his audacious undertaking, young Christian families should cultivate unwavering faith in God's providence. In times of trouble, remember that your faith has the potential to move figurative mountains in your life. Trusting that God is in control, even when situations seem insurmountable, can provide a profound sense of peace and resilience.

2. **Fasting as Spiritual Discipline:** St. Simon's practice of fasting to prepare for his monumental task is a reminder of the spiritual benefits of self-discipline.

Consider incorporating fasting into your family's routine to draw closer to God in facing challenges. Fasting can help you refocus your priorities, strengthen your connection with the divine, and gain clarity amid life's storms.

3. **The Power of Collective Prayer:** St. Simon's fervent prayers and the echoing cry of "Kyrie Eleison" demonstrate the transformative power of collective prayer. As a family, gather together in prayer, not only seeking divine intervention but also finding solace and unity in communing with God. Praying together as a family can strengthen your bond and provide comfort during times of trouble.

4. **Embrace Perseverance:** The story of St. Simon exemplifies the principle of perseverance in the face of adversity. Young families may encounter insurmountable challenges, but remember that the journey toward overcoming these challenges often requires steadfast determination. With God's guidance, you can navigate hardships and emerge stronger on the other side.

5. **Trusting God's Timing:** St. Simon's story teaches us that the manifestation of miracles often unfolds according to God's timing. Similarly, young families should remember that God's plans may not align with their own expectations. Trust that God's timing is perfect, and be patient as you navigate the challenges.

6. **Anchoring in Spiritual Practices:** Just as St. Simon relied on spiritual practices to fortify his faith, young families can anchor themselves in prayer, scripture reading, attending church, and participating in sacraments. These practices provide a steady foundation in the face of life's storms and remind you of the ever-present support of your Christian community.

7. **Perceiving Mountains as Opportunities:** While young families may not face literal mountains, they do encounter metaphorical challenges that can feel just as daunting. St. Simon's story invites you to see these challenges as opportunities for growth and transformation. Approach each difficulty with the belief that, through faith, you have the power to overcome and learn valuable lessons along the way.

As you navigate life's challenges, draw inspiration from St. Simon the Tanner's remarkable experience. While moving mountains may remain a miracle of the past, the recipe of faith, fasting, prayer, and trust in God's plan remains timeless and applicable to the challenges faced by young Christian families today. Just as St. Simon's faith reshaped the landscape around him, your faith can reshape the course of your journey, guiding you toward a life anchored in God's grace and guidance.

The Story of George Müller: George Müller, a 19th-century Christian evangelist and director of orphanages, is a testament to the harmonious blend of faith and practicality. Despite facing dire financial challenges to support the orphanages he cared for, Müller never asked for donations but relied solely on prayer and faith in God's provision.

On one occasion, with no food and funds available for breakfast, Müller led the children in prayer, thanking God for the meal they would receive. Shortly after their prayer, a baker knocked on the door, offering them freshly baked bread. Moments later, a milkman's cart broke down near the orphanage, and he offered them his milk to prevent spoilage.

George Müller's life showcased that faith isn't devoid of practical actions. His reliance on God's provision was coupled with the practicality of running the orphanages effectively. His legacy inspires us to trust God while also acting responsibly.

Wisdom for Everyday Living: *"The heart of the prudent acquires knowledge, and the ear of the wise seeks knowledge"*

(Proverbs 18:15).

Balancing faith and practicality require a wise approach to daily decisions. Just as faith informs our spiritual choices, practical wisdom guides our choices in the material realm. Seeking knowledge helps us make balanced decisions, honouring both aspects of our Christian walk.

Stewardship with eternal perspective: *"And He said to them, 'You are those who justify yourselves before men, but God knows your hearts. For what is highly esteemed among men is an abomination in the sight of God'"* (Luke 16:15).

In balancing faith and practicality, we must evaluate what we prioritise. Jesus' words remind us that earthly values can misalign with God's perspective. Stewardship of resources—faithfully managing what we have—requires an eternal perspective.

The dance between faith and practicality shapes our journey as Christians. We find that faith and practicality are not opposing forces but complementary aspects of our walk with God. By nurturing a faith that moves mountains, ensuring our faith is accompanied by works, seeking wisdom for everyday living, and stewarding resources with an eternal perspective, we achieve a harmony that reflects our commitment to living out our beliefs in the real world.

As we conclude our exploration of the delicate balance between faith and practicality, we shift our focus to a theme that resonates deeply with the human experience – weathering the storms of life while maintaining our steadfast faith. In Chapter 13, 'Finding Balance in the Storm,' we delve into the challenges that arise when life's trials test the very foundation of our beliefs. Drawing inspiration from the biblical narratives of courage, endurance, and unwavering faith, we'll uncover how our journey towards equilibrium is not exempt from the storms but instead empowered by them. Join us as we navigate the storms of life with the hope that anchors our souls, seeking the equilibrium that emerges from trust in the divine amidst life's tumultuous seas.

Chapter 13

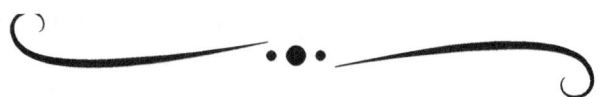

Finding Balance in the Storm

Life's journey often leads us through storms—sudden trials that test our faith and endurance. In these tempests, our ability to maintain balance becomes an art of profound significance. Navigating through turbulent times while holding onto our faith and practical wisdom is a challenge, but it is also an opportunity to witness the transformative power of God's presence. This chapter delves into the timeless teachings of Scripture that guide us through life's storms and shares stories of those who found unshakable balance amid adversity.

An Anchor for the Soul: In the heart of life's storms, our faith becomes an unyielding anchor for our soul. As the book of Hebrews eloquently expresses, our hope in Christ serves as this anchor—firm and secure—and ensures our stability even during crashing waves. This image reminds us that our trust in God provides unwavering certainty, allowing us to maintain equilibrium when everything around us seems to be in chaos.

Peace Beyond Understanding: Amid life's storms, the apostle Paul's words in Philippians offer a sanctuary of peace. "Be anxious for nothing, but in everything by prayer and supplication, with thanksgiving, let your requests be made known to God; and the peace of God, which surpasses all understanding, will guard your hearts and minds through Christ Jesus."(Philippians 4:6-8). This divine peace, a gift from God, surpasses our human comprehension. Through prayer, we connect with God, finding a tranquillity that guards our hearts and minds—a peace that enables us to navigate the storm gracefully.

St. Paul's Resolute Faith: The legacy of St. Paul echoes through time, an embodiment of unyielding faith amid tribulation. He writes to Timothy, "For I am already being poured out as a drink offering, and the time of my departure is at hand. I have fought the good fight, I have finished the race, I have kept the faith. Finally, there is laid up for me the crown of righteousness, which the Lord, the righteous Judge, will give to me on that Day, and not to me only but also to all who have loved His appearing." (2 Timothy 4:6-8) In these powerful words, we find a life lived with balance and unwavering conviction. St. Paul's steadfastness encourages us to stand firm in our faith even when confronted by the storms of life.

The Fiery Furnace of Faith: The story of Shadrach, Meshach, and Abed-Nego facing the fiery furnace in the book of Daniel resonates as an emblem of unwavering faith. Confronted with the choice of compromising their beliefs or facing a brutal fate, they chose to remain faithful to God. Their unshakable trust in God's deliverance amid the flames demonstrates the essence of balance—an unwavering commitment to God while placing their trust in His divine intervention.

The Light amidst Darkness: In the heart of Alexandria, a city with a rich history deeply intertwined with the Coptic Orthodox faith, a tragic event unfolded—a stark reminder of the ongoing battle between darkness and light. The **Elkedeseen Church,** The Saints Church, a sanctuary of worship and unity, was targeted by a merciless act of terrorism. Lives were lost, families shattered, and a community left in mourning. The shockwaves of this heinous act reverberated through the streets of Alexandria and across the hearts of believers worldwide.

Amid the intense rubble and the palpable atmosphere of grief, a remarkable phenomenon emerged that would forever echo the enduring strength of faith. Despite the profound pain and anger that surged within the Coptic Orthodox community, they responded with a resolute defiance against the darkness that sought to engulf them.

The world witnessed an extraordinary display of unity, love, and unwavering faith. Instead of succumbing to hatred or seeking vengeance, the people chose the path of forgiveness. This act of forgiveness, so deeply rooted in their Christian identity, sent shockwaves of its own—ones that transcended boundaries, cultures, and religions. It was a radiant manifestation of the light of Christ amidst the darkest of times.

The families who lost loved ones, their hearts heavy with grief, spoke words of love and forgiveness that resonated with the entire world. Their voices were not those of revenge or bitterness but rather of unwavering faith in the God of love and mercy. This response was a living testimony to their deep trust in God's plan, even in the face of the most unimaginable tragedy.

The Coptic Orthodox community didn't retreat in fear or anger but stood firm, united, and resilient. They refused to let the darkness define them. In their sorrow, they found solace in prayer and steadfast commitment to their faith. The sacred hymns that had echoed within the walls of their church for generations continued to be sung even louder and more persistent than before. It was as if the very stones of the church cried out, "We will not be silenced."

In the aftermath of the attack, the city of Alexandria witnessed an outpouring of support and solidarity from people of all backgrounds. A powerful message was sent—that the darkness of hatred and violence would not prevail over the light of love, compassion, and faith. The community's response became a testament to the power of faith in the face of adversity.

Amidst this storm, the Coptic Orthodox community, many of them very simple people, found their balance. They leaned on their unwavering faith, drawing strength from their shared history, deep-rooted traditions, and unbreakable connection to God. Their response was a living embodiment of Christ's teachings to love our enemies, forgive, and let His light shine in even the world's darkest corners.

The tragic event in Alexandria is a stark reminder that the world is not immune to darkness, but it also stands as a testament to the unyielding light of faith. The response of the Coptic Orthodox community became a beacon of hope, a symbol of resistance against hatred, and a reminder that even in the face of the darkest storms, the light of Christ will always prevail. Through their unwavering faith and resolute commitment to forgiveness and love, they showed the world that darkness may cast its shadow but can never extinguish the radiant light of faith.

Balancing Amidst Life's Storms: The art of maintaining balance during life's storms is a blend of faith and practicality. The anchor of hope, the peace that transcends understanding, St. Paul's resolute example, and the narrative of Shadrach, Meshach, and Abed-Nego inspire us to stand strong in the face of adversity. By embracing these principles, we find our equilibrium—anchored in faith, guided by divine wisdom, and unwavering trust in God's providence.

In embracing our Coptic Orthodox heritage, we can draw strength from the lives of saints who demonstrated steadfastness amid tribulations. Just as they found balance by clinging to their faith, prayer, and trust in God's plan, we, too, can navigate the storms of our lives. Our journey is not solitary; we walk alongside those who have gone before us and discover the enduring equilibrium in God's eternal love and grace.

Amid life's storms, as we strive to find balance and navigate the challenges that come our way, we realise the transformative power of our faith. In our pursuit of equilibrium, we now transition to a topic that touches the very core of our Christian values – 'The Challenge of Cultivating Love in a World Lacking Love.' As we delve into the complexities of a world that often falls short of displaying genuine love, we'll explore how our faith calls us to receive love and be active vessels of love, spreading compassion, empathy, and kindness to counter the prevailing indifference. Join us as we uncover the teachings of Christ that guide us in cultivating love even in the most challenging circumstances.

Chapter 14

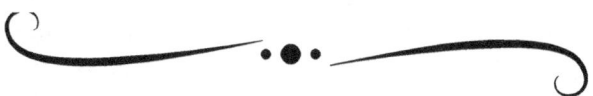

The Challenge of Cultivating Love in a World Lacking Love

Father Matta El-Meskeen, also known as Matthew the Poor, was a Coptic Orthodox monk and spiritual teacher who emphasised the importance of love and compassion in the Christian life. He often spoke about the transformative power of love and how it can influence our relationships and interactions with others.

Father Matta wrote in one of his teachings, "Cultivating love in our world is not merely a sentimental feeling, but a deliberate choice we make every day. Love is the essence of Christianity, for it is through love that we reflect the image of God in our lives. Love does not discriminate; it reaches out to friends and strangers, transcending boundaries, and barriers. When we cultivate love, we create an atmosphere of healing, understanding, and unity. Through love, we become true witnesses of Christ's message and contribute to the transformation of our world."

How ironic that this quote was written by Matta El-Meskeen more than 70 years ago when love was still flourishing and rich in our world!

Cultivating love has become a pressing challenge in a world marked by division and animosity. The absence of genuine Christian love hinders our relationships, communities, and family unity. This subsection digs into the call to cultivate love as Christians, drawing insights from Scripture and exploring the transformative power of love amid a love-deprived world.

The Greatest Commandment: *"And you shall love the Lord your God with all your heart, with all your soul, with all your mind, and with all your strength.' This is the first commandment. And the second, like it, is this: 'You shall love your neighbour as yourself.' There is no other commandment greater than these"* (Mark 12:30-31).

Our Lord Jesus' words underscore the paramount importance of love. Loving God with our entire being and loving our neighbours as ourselves encapsulate the essence of Christian living. This commandment directly addresses the challenge of cultivating love in a world that often neglects it.

Love Covers Multitudes: *"And above all things have fervent love for one another, for 'love will cover a multitude of sins'"* (1 Peter 4:8).

Love has the capacity to cover a multitude of offences. When we cultivate genuine love, we extend grace and forgiveness to one another, mending broken relationships and fostering unity. This verse encourages us to approach the challenge of love with fervour.

Love in Action: *"Let love be without hypocrisy. Abhor what is evil. Cling to what is good"* (Romans 12:9).

St. Paul's exhortation in Romans 12 emphasises the practicality of love. Love isn't mere sentiment—it's a conscious choice and decision to pursue goodness and reject evil. Our commitment to love without hypocrisy is a transformative testament in a world lacking love.

Lessons from the Early Monastic Fathers

St. Anthony and the Melody of Love: St. Anthony the Great, one of the earliest Christian monks, radiated love through his life of asceticism. In the desert, he encountered a group of monks who questioned how they could attain the heights of spiritual virtue. St. Anthony responded by directing them to a beautiful melody sung by a group of birds. He told them that as each bird's note harmonises with the others, so should their hearts resonate with the melody of divine love. St. Anthony's lesson highlighted that true spiritual growth and unity stem from cultivating genuine love for God and one another.

Allow me to share a heartfelt story about a beloved saint who holds a special place in my heart. His teachings have touched my soul deeply, and I am eager to delve into his writings, particularly the fifty homilies he composed. This saint is none other than the illustrious Saint Macarius the Great.

St. Macarius the Great's Act of Love: St. Macarius the Great once beseeched the Lord to show him someone who mirrored his own spiritual journey. In response, a celestial voice proclaimed, "Two women are comparable in this and that city." With divine guidance, he embarked on a journey with his cane of palm branches to seek out these extraordinary souls.

Arriving at their dwelling, he knocked on their door, and one of the women emerged, bowing to the ground in prostration upon seeing the venerable older man. Unaware of his identity, she paid him homage, just as the two women had witnessed their husbands do for strangers. The other woman, recognising the saint, set her son down and humbly approached him, offering water for him to wash his feet and preparing a table for his meal.

With an air of purpose, the saint revealed his divine mission to them. He expressed his intention to partake in their hospitality only if they shared the intimate details of their relationship with God, for he had been sent to them by God himself. Curious yet reverent, they inquired, "Who are you, our father?" He answered, "I am Maqara, who dwells in the wilderness of Skete."

Upon hearing his identity, they were overcome with awe and emotion. Rising from their prostration, they acknowledged their own sinfulness and inquired about the deeds he sought from them. In response, St. Macarius the Great humbly implored them, "For God's sake, I came to you with exhaustion, so do not withhold from me the spiritual benefit of my soul."

In genuine humility, the women disclosed their extraordinary way of life. Despite being sisters-in-law, they had married two brothers. They were denied when they sought permission from their husbands to join a convent. Determined to remain steadfast, they made a sacred pact to cultivate a bond of divine love. They practised perpetual fasting and unceasing prayer until evening, nurturing their souls.

Remarkably, each woman nursed the other's child as her own, mirroring a profound maternal unity. Even their husbands, goats, and sheep shepherds were welcomed into their spiritual haven with the same reverence as the holy brothers James and John. They exhibited diligent charity and mercy towards strangers, shunning all worldly conversations and behaviours.

Humbled by these women's virtuous lives, St. Macarius left their presence, overcome by a deep sense of repentance and awe. He beat his chest and slapped his face, repeating, "Woe, woe, woe, woe, woe, woe, woe, woe to me!" Their story is a radiant testimony to the transformative power of divine love, unity, and devotion, inspiring generations to embrace a life rooted in humility and pursuing God's truth.

In a world that sometimes prioritises self-interest and material gain, the challenge of cultivating and nurturing love within young Christian families becomes increasingly significant. The absence of genuine love and compassion in society can cast a shadow over couples' efforts to build strong, harmonious relationships.

Understanding the Challenge: In a world driven by individualism and instant gratification, selfless love can often be overshadowed. The emphasis on personal achievements, societal pressures, and the pursuit of external validation can lead to a culture that undervalues the beauty of sacrificial love that Christ exemplified.

Impact on Relationships: The lack of love in the world can affect young Christian families in several ways:

- Expectation vs. Reality: Couples may enter marriage with unrealistic expectations based on societal norms and media portrayals of love, leading to disappointment when faced with the reality of everyday challenges.
- Communication Breakdown: The absence of love in broader interactions can impact how couples communicate. A lack of empathy and compassion can hinder effective communication and lead to misunderstandings.
- Influence on Parenting: The societal lack of love can affect parenting approaches. Couples may struggle to model Christ-like love to their children amid conflicting messages from the world.

Addressing the Challenge:

- **Start at Home:** Encourage each other to create a nurturing and loving environment within your own family. By embodying Christ-like love in your interactions, set a powerful example for your children and others around you.

- **Practice Selflessness:** Discuss with each other the importance of putting others' needs before one's own. Emphasise that selfless love requires sacrifice and an attitude of servanthood, mirroring Christ's love for humanity.

- **Community Engagement:** Encourage each other to engage in acts of kindness and compassion within your community. Volunteering, supporting charitable initiatives, and reaching out to those in need can spread love beyond their immediate family.

- **Prayer and Faith:** Remind each other that a strong foundation of faith can provide the spiritual resources needed to overcome the challenges of a love-deficient world. Regular prayer, Scripture reading, and involvement in a supportive church community can reinforce your commitment to love.

- **Reframe Perspectives:** Help each other shift your focus from seeking external validation to finding fulfilment in living out Christ's love. You can find true joy in your relationships by seeking validation from God rather than the people around you.

- **Educate Children:** Discuss with each other the importance of instilling values of love, empathy, and compassion in children from an early age. Always adopt and learn strategies for fostering a loving environment that encourages these qualities to flourish.

The Challenge of Cultivating Love in a World Lacking Love

Pope Shenouda III, the beloved spiritual leader of the Coptic Orthodox Church, imparted, *"Love never fails. Love is the bond that ties us together."* His words echo the essence of Christ's teachings and inspire us to persevere in cultivating love, even in a world that often falls short of it.

Cultivating love in a love-deficient world is both a challenge and a divine calling. We counteract the world's scarcity of genuine love as we heed the greatest commandments, embrace love that covers multitudes, and let our love manifest in actions. The Coptic stories of St. Anthony, the harmonious melody of divine love, and the transformative journeys of St. Moses the Black and St. Macarius the Great echo the lessons of Scripture. By nurturing love as Christ did, we become beacons of hope and agents of transformation, catalysing a ripple effect of love in a world hungry for it.

In the pursuit of our journey through the challenge of cultivating love in a world often lacking love, we recognise the profound impact love has on our lives as Christians. Love is the cornerstone of our faith, guiding our actions and relationships in a world that desperately needs it. Now, as we transition to our next chapter, 'Nurturing Balanced Children in a Complex World,' we focus on raising children who can thrive in a rapidly changing and often confusing world. Join us as we explore how to instil values, resilience, and a strong sense of faith in our children, equipping them to navigate life's complexities while grounded in God's love.

Chapter 15

Nurturing Balanced Children in a Complex World by empowering them

Raising children in today's intricate world presents an array of challenges. The dynamic interplay of culture, technology, rewritten values, and societal norms can shape their perspectives, beliefs, and values. This subsection – among the longest sections in the book due to the utmost importance of this challenge in raising our children in today's environment - explores the essential task of nurturing balanced children, drawing wisdom from Scripture to guide parents in fostering a holistic upbringing that equips them for life's complexities. Also, empowering and guiding them to make sound decisions aligned with their deeply cemented Christian values.

Navigating the world's complexities requires nurturing, balanced children equipped with faith, discernment, and love. By teaching them the way to go, setting virtuous examples, cultivating wisdom through a relationship with God, and offering gentle guidance, parents empower their children to become resilient individuals who positively impact the world around them.

Raising balanced children in today's world is a challenge that weighs heavily on the hearts of young Christian families. The rapid pace of change, the abundance of information, and the complexity of societal pressures make it crucial for parents to provide their children with a strong foundation that embraces faith and wisdom.

Nurturing and raising balanced kids means balance and beyond: In the intricate tapestry of our modern world, nurturing balanced Christian children is a profound responsibility that resonates deeply with parents and guardians. As we guide the young hearts and minds entrusted to our care by God, we're called to foster an environment that cultivates harmony between their spiritual growth, personal development, and engagement with the complexities of our rapidly evolving society while deeply cemented in their faith, traditions, and the bible teachings.

Balancing Faith and Modernity: Navigating the complexities of the contemporary world can be challenging, particularly when raising children deeply rooted in their Christian faith and church life. In a digital age where information flows incessantly, and societal values may diverge from those of the Gospel, striking a balance between faith and modernity becomes imperative. It requires a delicate dance—an intentional weaving of traditional Christian principles with the demands of an ever-changing landscape.

Guidance from Scripture: In nurturing balanced Christian children, Scripture provides invaluable insights. Proverbs 22:6 (NKJV) advises, "Train up a child in the way he should go, and when he is old, he will not depart from it." This timeless wisdom reminds us of the significance of early guidance, shaping the foundations upon which children build their lives.

Faith in Action: Fostering balance involves imparting faith knowledge and demonstrating faith in action. When children witness parents and caregivers living out their faith with authenticity, compassion, and humility, they learn the profound impact of aligning belief with behaviour.

How to Deal with mistakes and failure in our children: Dealing with mistakes and failure in our children is a crucial aspect of parenting that needs special skills and attention, if we are to expose them to the world with discernment, how do we help them when/if they fall? I am a big advocate of learning from failures in life! All the men and women of God in the Holy bible committed very costly mistakes that cost hefty price tags! But look at the way God acknowledges, corrects, each one and coaches them in order that they learn!! And probably you and I too, my friend has done the same in our lives, big failures, big mistakes and great lessons... part of gaining priceless wisdom! Here are some strategies on how to deal with mistakes:

1. **Creating a Safe Environment:** It's essential for children to know that home is a safe place to make mistakes. Parents should foster an environment where children feel comfortable sharing their weaknesses and failures without fear of harsh judgment or punishment. This encourages open communication.

2. **Teaching Resilience:** Mistakes and failures are valuable learning opportunities. Parents can help their children develop resilience by encouraging them to view failures as stepping stones to success. Discussing stories of famous individuals who faced failures before achieving greatness can be inspiring.

3. **Avoiding Overprotection:** While it's natural to want to shield children from disappointment, it's essential to strike a balance. Overprotecting them can hinder their ability to develop problem-solving skills and

resilience. Parents should allow children to face age-appropriate challenges.

4. **Encouraging Responsibility:** Parents can teach children to take responsibility for their mistakes. This involves acknowledging the error, understanding its consequences, and working towards a solution or improvement.

5. **Modelling Acceptance of Failure:** Children often learn by example. When parents openly share their own experiences of failure and how they overcame them, it helps children see that it's a normal part of life.

6. **Setting Realistic Expectations:** It's crucial for parents to have realistic expectations for their children. Unrealistic pressure to succeed can lead to anxiety and fear of failure. Parents should acknowledge their child's unique strengths and weaknesses.

7. **Emphasizing Effort over Outcome:** Instead of focusing solely on outcomes or grades, parents can highlight the importance of effort and hard work. Praising the process of trying and learning can motivate children to persevere despite setbacks.

8. **Providing Support:** Parents should let their children know that they're there to support them, both emotionally and practically. Whether it's helping with homework or providing emotional support after a disappointment, this reassurance is crucial.

9. **Teaching Problem-Solving Skills:** Parents can guide their children in problem-solving techniques. Encouraging them to think critically about how to address and learn from their mistakes empowers them to handle similar situations better in the future.

10. **Offering Unconditional Love:** Regardless of their children's mistakes or failures, parents should convey

that their love is unconditional. Children need to feel secure in their parents' love, even when they stumble.

Cultivating Critical Thinking: Balanced Christian children are equipped with the ability to think critically and discern truth in a world inundated with information. Encourage open discussions where they can explore their questions, doubts, and curiosities within the framework of their faith. This practice fosters a deep understanding of their beliefs and prepares them to face challenges confidently.

Prayerful Foundation: A life of prayer becomes the cornerstone of nurturing balanced Christian children. Teaching them the power of prayer, both individually and as a family, fosters a sense of connection with God and reliance on His guidance in all aspects of life.

Engaging Culture with Discernment: In a world that often celebrates values contrary to those of the Gospel, encourage children to engage with popular culture, media, and technology through a lens of discernment. Help them recognise the elements aligning with their faith and those requiring scrutiny or avoidance.

Service and Empathy: Balanced Christian children understand the call to serve others and exhibit empathy. Engaging in acts of kindness, volunteering, and supporting those in need instils a sense of responsibility and compassion that aligns with the teachings of Christ.

Adapting Traditions: As we raise children in a constantly evolving world, adapting traditional practices to resonate with contemporary realities becomes essential. Blend time-honoured Christian traditions with innovative ways of expressing faith, allowing children to engage meaningfully with their heritage while embracing the present dynamics. One of the most influential Orthodox theologians and churchmen in the West during the 20th century, particularly in the field of liturgical theology, Fr. Alexander Schmemann who became dean of St. Vladimir's Orthodox Theological Seminary in New York quoted *"The true orthodox way of thought has always been historical, has always included the past, but has never been enslaved by it. . . [for] the strength of the Church is not in the past, present, or future, but in Christ"*

The Church, as we should expect of any historical phenomenon, had changed and developed through the centuries. True enough. Still, the Church in its essential identity - in its organic and spiritual continuity - remains substantially coextensive with the Church of the Apostles. It is, in effect, nothing less than the living continuation in time and space of the primitive Church in Jerusalem. It can be viewed as the one Catholic Church in all its fullness and plenitude. Orthodox worship, for example, is nothing less than a witness to history; it recalls, in all its rich diversity, particular historical events not only from the earthly life of the Lord, but from the life of the Church, its saints, ascetics, martyrs, and theologians.

Living with Purpose: Above all, nurturing balanced Christian children involves instilling a sense of purpose aligned with God's plan. Proverbs 16:3 (NKJV) encapsulates this beautifully: "Commit your works to the Lord, and your thoughts will be established." By empowering children to commit to God's purpose, we guide them toward a balanced existence where faith, values, and actions harmonise.

Remember that you are not alone in nurturing balanced Christian children in today's complex world. Draw strength from the supportive Christian family, friends, and community around you, and lean on the unchanging truths of Scripture. By intentionally nurturing their faith, character, and engagement with the world, you lay a foundation that equips them to navigate life's complexities with wisdom, grace, and an unwavering commitment to their Christian identity.

Children as Arrows: *"Like arrows in the hand of a warrior, so are the children of one's youth"* (Psalm 127:4).

The analogy of children as arrows highlights their potential to be guided and aimed purposefully. As parents, we are entrusted with shaping and directing our children's lives, preparing them to navigate the world's complexities with wisdom and discernment.

Teach the Way: *"Train up a child in the way he should go, and when he is old he will not depart from it"* (Proverbs 22:6).

Proverbs emphasises the significance of early guidance. By instilling values rooted in faith and integrity, parents lay a foundation to guide their children through life's intricacies.

Imitation of Virtue: *"And you became followers of us and of the Lord, having received the word in much affliction, with joy of the Holy Spirit, so that you became examples to all in Macedonia and Achaia who believe"* (1 Thessalonians 1:6-7).

Saint Paul's words to the Thessalonians underscore the power of setting an example. As parents, we play a pivotal role in modelling virtues, demonstrating how to navigate challenges, and exhibiting a balanced approach to life.

Cultivating Wisdom: *"The fear of the Lord is the beginning of wisdom, and the knowledge of the Holy One is understanding"* (Proverbs 9:10).

True wisdom begins with reverence for God. Teaching children to prioritise their relationship with God lays a strong foundation for navigating the world's complexities with discernment.

Parental Guidance and Love: *"And you, fathers, do not provoke your children to wrath, but bring them up in the training and admonition of the Lord"* (Ephesians 6:4).

Ephesians emphasises the dual role of guidance and love. Parents are called to nurture their children's growth through gentle guidance, fostering an environment where faith and wisdom flourish.

Understanding the Challenge: Modern society bombards children with influences that can lead them astray from the values their parents hold dear. Materialism, instant gratification, exposure to conflicting ideologies, and the allure of technology can disrupt the delicate balance parents strive to establish in their children's upbringing.

Impact on Parenting: The challenge of raising balanced children can manifest in various ways:

- **Navigating Technology:** The omnipresence of technology can impede children's development of real-world social skills and create a disconnect between virtual and authentic experiences.
- **Value Confusion:** The myriad of messages children encounter can lead to confusion about core values. Parents might struggle to instil their beliefs in a way that resonates with children and withstands external influences.
- **Pressure to Conform:** Peer pressure and societal expectations can encourage children to conform to popular trends, potentially sidelining their spiritual growth and emotional well-being.

Addressing the Challenge: How can we empower young Christian parents to navigate the challenge of raising balanced children in today's intricate landscape?

- **Clear Communication:** Encourage open conversations with children about the values that underpin the family's faith. Discuss the world's complexities and equip them with the tools to assess conflicting messages critically.
- **Limiting Screen Time:** Discuss strategies for managing children's exposure to screens and the internet. Emphasise quality over quantity and encourage alternative activities that promote physical activity, creativity, and real-world interactions.

- **Modelling Balance:** Demonstrate a balanced life by setting healthy work, technology, and leisure boundaries. Children learn by example, so parents should display a well-rounded lifestyle that reflects the values they wish to instil.
- **Teaching Discernment:** Educate children about discernment – the ability to assess information critically, make informed choices, and embrace values aligned with their faith. Equip them with the tools to distinguish between what is beneficial and what is harmful.
- **Encouraging Spiritual Growth:** Prioritise a solid spiritual foundation. Regular family devotions, attending church services, and engaging in age-appropriate discussions about faith can give children a sense of grounding.
- **Fostering Independence:** Nurture children's ability to make sound decisions while respecting their individuality. Teach them problem-solving skills, encourage them to ask questions, and provide a safe space for exploration.
- **Community and Mentoring:** Connect with like-minded families in our faith, values, and beliefs and involve children in church activities to cultivate a sense of community. Encourage relationships with mentors who can provide guidance and support beyond parental influence.
- **Sunday School role:** Develop the habit and encourage children to attend, belong and love Sunday school. The Role of Sunday School within the church community plays a vital role in nurturing balanced children. Children receive a solid foundation in faith, values, and biblical wisdom through age-appropriate teachings, interactive lessons, and Christian fellowship. Sunday

School complements parental guidance by providing a structured environment where children can deepen their understanding of God's word and build relationships with peers who share.

Empowering Children in Nurturing Balanced Lives: In raising balanced children, empowerment goes beyond mere instruction. It fosters their capacity to think critically, make informed decisions, and embrace their identity as young Christians in a multifaceted world. Empowering children with faith-driven discernment is a transformative journey that equips them to walk steadfastly through life's challenges.

Empowerment also emerges from weaving prayer into the fabric of their lives. Teaching children the power of prayer, both individually and collectively, anchors their hearts to God's wisdom and guidance. Through prayer, children learn to seek divine insight in their decision-making, fostering a reliance on God's presence in their journey.

Ultimately, empowerment culminates in guiding children to find purpose aligned with God's plan. Empower them to commit to God's purpose, aligning their thoughts, actions, and aspirations with His divine harmony. This empowers them to navigate life's intricacies with resilience and an unwavering commitment to their Christian identity.

As you embark on the empowering journey of raising balanced children in today's complex world, **remember that you are not alone.** Draw strength from your faith, family, and the supportive Christian community. By intentionally empowering your children with faith, wisdom, and discernment, you provide them with the tools to confidently navigate life's complexities while standing firm in their Christian values.

Teach the Way: The timeless wisdom of Proverbs 22:6 advises parents to train their children in the path they should follow. By instilling values rooted in faith and integrity, parents lay a foundation that guides their children throughout the intricate journey of life.

Imitation of Virtue: Following the example of Saint Paul's words to the Thessalonians, parents can empower their children by exemplifying virtues in their own lives. By doing so, parents become living examples of faith, resilience, and balanced living, providing a roadmap for their children to navigate the world's challenges.

Cultivating Wisdom: True wisdom begins with a reverence for God. Empowering children to prioritise their relationship with God fosters a deep well of discernment, helping them navigate the world's complexities with clarity and purpose.

In the journey of empowering children to lead balanced lives within a complex world, **remember that you are shaping the next generation.** By imbuing them with faith, wisdom, and the ability to discern, you are preparing them to thrive amidst the challenges they will inevitably encounter. Your guidance empowers them to embrace their identity as young Christians, inspiring them to make choices that reflect their values and positively impact the world around them.

Teaching Children to Make Godly Decisions: It is a sacred responsibility to guide children to make decisions rooted in their Christian faith. Here are ways to instil godly decision-making principles in their hearts:

1. **Biblical Values:** Introduce children to biblical values and teachings that serve as the foundation for their choices. Share stories of characters in the Bible and the saints from our rich church Synaxarium, who made honourable decisions, emphasising virtues like love, integrity, compassion, and humility.

2. **Prayerful Guidance:** Teach children the significance of seeking God's guidance through prayer. Encourage them to pray about decisions, inviting the Holy Spirit to lead them in making choices that align with God's

will.
3. **Moral Consequences:** Discuss the moral consequences of decisions in the context of God's commandments. Help children understand how their choices can either honour or deviate from God's life plan.
4. **Role of Scripture:** Use relevant Bible verses to illustrate the importance of wise decisions. Scriptures like Proverbs 3:5-6 and James 1:5 emphasise seeking God's wisdom and trusting in Him for guidance.
5. **Virtuous Living:** Demonstrate a life of virtue and integrity through your own choices. Children learn by example, so they exhibit humility, honesty, and selflessness in decision-making.

Equipping children with the ability to make godly decisions involves practical training that reflects Christ-centred values. Here's how you can train them to make decisions in alignment with their Christian faith:

1. **Choices within Boundaries:** Provide children with choices within the framework of Christian principles. For instance, let them decide how to use their time, talents, and resources to serve others or honour God.
2. **Biblical Discernment:** Teach children to discern God's voice by comparing their decisions with biblical teachings. Encourage them to ask questions like, "Does this choice reflect God's love and truth?"
3. **Reflection and Prayer:** Teach children to reflect on their decisions through prayer and self-examination. Help them consider how their choices align with the teachings of Christ and the fruit of the Spirit.
4. **Fruits of the Spirit:** Introduce the fruits of the Spirit (Galatians 5:22-23) as a guide for decision-making. Encourage them to consider whether their choices

exhibit love, joy, peace, patience, kindness, goodness, faithfulness, gentleness, and self-control.

5. **Service and Sacrifice:** Emphasise Christ's example of selfless service and sacrificial love. Encourage children to make decisions that prioritise the well-being of others and reflect Christ's character.

6. **Discussing Temptations:** Openly discuss challenges and temptations children may face. Equip them with scriptural knowledge and strategies to overcome these temptations while making decisions that honour God.

7. **Practice Critical Thinking:** Encourage children to think critically about various options before deciding. Ask thought-provoking questions that challenge them to consider different angles, potential outcomes, and ethical implications of their choices.

8. **Explain Consequences:** Help children understand that every decision has positive and negative consequences. Use relatable examples to illustrate how choices they make today can impact their lives in the future. This helps them think beyond the immediate and consider the long-term effects.

9. **Modelling Faith:** Let children witness your reliance on God's wisdom in your decisions. Share instances when you've sought God's guidance and experienced the blessings of following His lead.

10. **Share Personal Stories:** Share your experiences, successes, and failures where decisions were pivotal. Hearing real-life stories can help children grasp the complexity of decision-making and learn from your wisdom.

11. **Accountability:** Establish an atmosphere of accountability within the family. Encourage children to share their decisions with you, fostering open dialogue

about their thought processes and choices.

12. **Trust in God's Faithfulness:** Cultivating all of the above through instilling all the wisdom, fear and knowledge is one thing, and trusting in God's faithfulness is everything. Draw from your life experience with God, how God walked with your grandparents, parents and yourself and God will continue the journey with your kids.

By teaching and training children to make godly decisions, you're shaping their character and empowering them to live out their faith in a world that often challenges Christian values. As you walk alongside them on this journey, remember to continually point them to the source of all wisdom—God Himself.

Remember, the journey of teaching and training children to make good decisions is ongoing. Your guidance and support remain crucial as they encounter new situations and challenges. By instilling them with the values, critical thinking skills, and discernment they need, you empower them to navigate life's complexities with wisdom and confidence.

The challenge of raising balanced children in the modern world is formidable. Still, with intentional effort, young Christian parents can guide their children towards a life of balance, faith, and discernment. By equipping children with the tools to navigate complexities and make choices aligned with their values, parents help ensure that the next generation stands strong amidst the world's challenges, embracing the divine harmony that God intended.

As we conclude our exploration of nurturing balanced children amid a complex world, we recognise the importance of guiding the younger generation with wisdom, love, and a foundation rooted in Christian values. Providing them with the tools to navigate the challenges of this world is a testament to our commitment as parents to raise children who embrace faith, resilience, and discernment. Now, as we transition to our next chapter, 'Overcoming the Challenge of Comparisons in the Light of Christian Values,' we delve into the impactful topic of comparisons, exploring how we can overcome this common yet corrosive habit through the lens of our faith. Join us as we uncover the liberating truths that enable us to embrace contentment and find our worth in Christ alone.

PART THREE

NAVIGATING LIFE THROUGH CHRISTIAN VAUES

Chapter 16

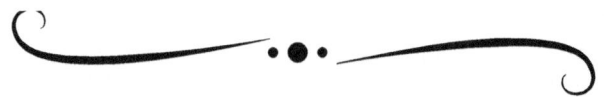

Overcoming the Challenge of Comparisons in the Light of Christian Values

Once upon a time, a young girl named Lily and her family lived in a serene village nestled between rolling hills and glistening rivers. The villagers were known for their harmonious lives and close-knit community, where each family was unique in its own way.

Lily's family consisted of her parents, two younger siblings, and a sprightly dog named Rusty. They lived in a quaint cottage on the outskirts of the village, surrounded by lush gardens and the soothing melody of chirping birds.

One day, the village received news of an enchanted forest deep within the hills. This forest was said to grant anyone who entered a single wish. News spread like wildfire, and families from the village began to venture into the forest with their hearts full of desires.

The Balance Beam

As weeks passed, stories of granted wishes spread throughout the village. Families returned with newfound riches, grand houses, and impressive possessions. Soon, whispers of comparison filled the air, and the enchanting forest became a hot topic of discussion in every home.

Lily's family, however, remained content with their simple life. They cherished their cosy cottage, enjoyed home-cooked meals, and spent evenings playing games and sharing stories. Lily's parents taught their children the value of gratitude and the importance of cherishing what they had.

One day, Lily decided to visit the enchanted forest, curious to see if it would fulfil her wishes. Deep within the woods, she came across an ancient oak tree with a shimmering aura. The tree spoke gently, "What is your wish, dear child?"

Lily thought momentarily and said, "I wish for my family to be the happiest in the village."

The tree smiled warmly and granted her wish. As Lily returned home, she noticed something magical. Her family's love and bond seemed to shine brighter than before. They laughed heartily, shared stories with even greater enthusiasm, and embraced each other's company with newfound appreciation.

The village continued to buzz with stories of wishes coming true, but Lily's family remained untouched by comparison. Their days were filled with love, joy, and gratitude and their hearts remained content.

As time passed, villagers started noticing the unique radiance of Lily's family. They marvelled at the laughter that echoed from their cottage and the warmth that emanated from their gatherings. Slowly but surely, families realised that true happiness wasn't found in grand possessions, but in the love and togetherness, they already possessed.

The enchanting forest gradually lost its allure, and the village turned its focus back to the values that had made it a close-knit community. Families learned that comparing themselves to others only diminished the beauty of their own lives.

And so, the village thrived once more, not with wishes granted by an enchanted forest but with the enchantment of gratitude, love, and contentment that radiated from Lily's family. They became a shining example of how true happiness is found within, and their story was passed down through generations as a reminder that the greatest treasures in life are often right before our eyes.

In today's world of social media and constant connectivity, the challenge of comparisons has intensified. Comparing ourselves to others can lead to discontentment and undermine our self-worth. Comparing Christian families to one another, whether it's their children, resources, achievements, or any other aspect, can be detrimental to the families involved and their relationships. Here's an elaboration on the dangers of such comparisons:

- **Undermining Contentment:** When Christian families constantly compare themselves to others, it can lead to a lack of contentment with their own blessings. Instead of being grateful for what they have, they might focus on what they lack compared to others. This undermines the principle of being thankful to God for His provision.

- **Fuelling Envy and Jealousy:** Comparison often leads to envy and jealousy. If one family seems to have more or achieve more than another, it can breed resentment and negative emotions. These feelings can poison relationships and hinder the spirit of brotherly love that should characterise Christian communities.

- **Unhealthy Competition:** Healthy competition can be motivating, but it becomes unhealthy when it becomes a constant race to outdo one another. Christian families should work together to support and uplift each other, not engage in cutthroat rivalry.

- **Strained Relationships:** Constant comparison can strain relationships between families. Instead of fostering a sense of unity and mutual support, families might become guarded and cautious around each other, fearing judgment or criticism.
- **Neglecting Individuality:** Every family is unique, with its own strengths, challenges, and circumstances. Comparing families ignores this individuality and reduces them to mere benchmarks for measurement. It fails to acknowledge the personal journeys that each family is on.
- **Impact on Children:** When children see their parents constantly comparing them to others, it can negatively affect their self-esteem and sense of worth. Children should be encouraged to develop their own talents and abilities without the pressure of constant comparison.
- **Distraction from Spiritual Growth:** The focus on comparing material or worldly achievements can divert attention from spiritual growth and development. Instead of striving to be more Christ-like, families might prioritise worldly success as the ultimate goal.
- **Loss of Genuine Relationships:** When families are more concerned with measuring up to others, genuine relationships can suffer. True fellowship is built on love, support, and empathy, not superficial comparisons.
- **Missed Opportunities for Learning:** Instead of learning from each other's experiences, strengths, and challenges, families might view each other solely through comparison. This prevents the sharing of wisdom and mutual growth.

- **Diminished Witness:** Christian families are called to be a light to the world, showing the love and unity that comes from faith. When internal comparison is rampant, it can tarnish this witness, portraying Christians as judgmental and competitive rather than loving and supportive.

In Christian communities, the focus should be on unity, love, and mutual edification. Instead of comparing themselves to others, families should encourage each other, celebrate one another's successes, and offer support in times of need. By embracing a spirit of humility, contentment, and gratitude, Christian families can create an environment where everyone can thrive without the weight of constant comparison.

Our Identity in Christ: *"For we are His workmanship, created in Christ Jesus for good works, which God prepared beforehand that we should walk in them"* (Ephesians 2:10).

Ephesians reminds us that our identity is rooted in being God's unique creation, crafted with purpose. Internalising this truth makes us less likely to measure our worth against others.

The Parable of the Prodigal Son: The parable of the prodigal son (Luke 15:11-32) illustrates the danger of comparing oneself to others. The elder son's comparison to his prodigal brother led to resentment. Embracing Christian values means recognising that each individual's journey is distinct and equally valued in the eyes of God.

Contentment and Godliness: *"Now godliness with contentment is great gain"* (1 Timothy 6:6). The verse emphasises the synergy between godliness and contentment. Focusing on our relationship with God and being content with what we have counteracts the comparison trap.

The Grumbling Israelites: The Israelites' constant comparison to their past circumstances while wandering in the desert led to dissatisfaction (Exodus 16:2-3). Instead of trusting God's provision, they fixated on what they lacked.

This story underscores the importance of gratitude and faith over comparison.

Rejoice in Others' Blessings: *"Rejoice with those who rejoice, and weep with those who weep"* (Romans 12:15). Romans encourage a mindset of empathy and shared joy. Instead of comparing, embracing others' victories, and supporting them fosters unity and love.

The challenge of comparisons is prevalent in our interconnected world, but as Christians, we can navigate it through the lens of our faith. By acknowledging our identity in Christ, learning from the parables of the prodigal son and the grumbling Israelites, pursuing contentment, and rejoicing in others' blessings, we shift our focus from comparison to gratitude and empathy. In doing so, we cultivate a healthier self-image and promote harmony in our relationships, aligning our lives with the values of our Christian faith.

The challenge of comparisons among young Christian families resonates deeply in today's social landscape. The prevalence of social media and societal expectations can lead to feelings of inadequacy and discontentment. Overcoming this challenge requires a strong foundation in Christian values, emphasising contentment, gratitude, and a focus on individual purpose.

Understanding the Challenge: Comparisons can create an unhealthy cycle of envy and self-doubt, particularly in a world where idealised portrayals of life are showcased on social media platforms. Young Christian families might find themselves measuring their achievements against those of others, leading to feelings of insecurity and a loss of focus on their own blessings.

Impact on Relationships:

The challenge of comparisons can impact young Christian families in several ways:
- **Dissatisfaction:** Constant comparisons can lead to discontentment, causing families to overlook the blessings and joys in their own lives.
- **Strained Relationships:** Couples might experience tension and disagreement as they strive to meet external expectations rather than nurture their unique partnership.
- **Parental Pressure:** Parents' desires to keep up with the perceived successes of other families can trickle down to their children, unintentionally instilling unhealthy expectations.

Addressing the Challenge:

- **Gratitude Practice:** Encourage your family to practice gratitude by regularly reflecting on the blessings they have. This can shift their focus from what they lack to what they've been given.
- **Limit Social Media:** Discuss the importance of using social media mindfully. Encourage families to remember that what is shared online often represents curated moments, not the entirety of someone's life. According to an expert clinical psychologist Michelle Tanious; "with social media, one thing I have noticed is not only is there a comparison with other families but there is a lot of information being disseminated by so-called "experts" on parenting topics. These all look lovely on the surface but I have seen many parents who are striving to be perfect according to these standards

and it is causing a lot of anxiety that they are not doing it right. They can set high expectations for themselves, are really disappointed by their child's behaviour because they see it as failure or experience frustration with their partners who aren't doing things their way.

- **Rejoice in Others' Successes:** Teach your family to genuinely celebrate others' successes and achievements rather than viewing them as threats. This attitude cultivates a spirit of unity and love.
- **Foster Self-Worth:** Help your family and each other to understand that their worth is not determined by external comparisons but by their identity in Christ. Emphasise the inherent value each family member possesses.
- **Embrace Uniqueness:** Guide each other to recognise their own uniqueness. Every family's journey is different, and God has a unique purpose for each one.
- **Focus on Purpose:** Encourage your family members to identify and focus on their own purpose and calling. By striving to fulfil their God-given mission, they can find fulfilment and satisfaction without comparing themselves to others.
- **Community of Support:** Cultivate a nurturing community within the church, fostering a gathering of young families that provides a safe space for open discussions about their challenges, victories, and difficulties. Through this sense of camaraderie, families can combat the sense of isolation that often arises from comparisons. A few years back, I was privileged to attend a remarkable conference organised for young families' service, "One Flesh Fellowship" in Melbourne. This experience personally inspired me and ignited a strong passion to engage with young families as they navigate the complexities of modern

lifestyle challenges.

The challenge of comparisons among young Christian families is formidable, but it can be overcome with a steadfast commitment to Christian values. By anchoring their actions in gratitude and contentment and focusing on their unique purpose, families can rise above the pressures of comparison and cultivate a sense of joy and fulfilment in their journey. Through Christ-centred guidance, they can learn to appreciate the beauty of their own lives without being overshadowed by external expectations.

As we conclude our exploration of overcoming the detrimental habit of comparisons, we recognise the transformative power of embracing contentment and gratitude in our lives. Turning our gaze away from the allure of comparison and towards the richness of our blessings is a step towards living with the joy and freedom that Christ offers. As we transition to our next chapter, 'Pursuing Wealth in Alignment with Christian Principles,' we delve into the intricate topic of wealth and its place in the Christian journey. Join us as we navigate the complexities of financial prosperity, stewardship, and the pursuit of treasures that endure beyond this world.

Chapter 17

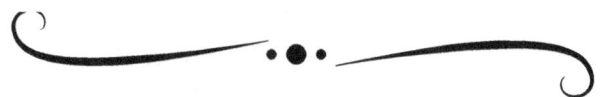

Pursuing Wealth in Alignment with Christian Principles

The pursuit of wealth is a common aspiration in today's materialistic society. However, as Christians, our pursuit of wealth should be guided by principles that align with our faith. This subsection examines pursuing wealth in light of Christian values, drawing insights from biblical stories, scriptures, the wisdom of early church fathers, and a story from the Coptic Church to provide a balanced perspective.

"Now godliness with contentment is great gain." **1Timothy 6:6**

This verse beautifully encapsulates the profound connection between godliness and contentment. It serves as a reminder that true richness lies not in accumulating material possessions or pursuing worldly desires but in aligning our hearts with the divine.

Godliness and Its Significance: Godliness is characterised by devotion to God, righteous living, and an earnest desire to reflect His character. It is intentionally cultivating a relationship with the Creator, where His wisdom and love guide our thoughts, actions, and intentions. Godliness encourages us to seek holiness, humility, and selflessness, mirroring the life of Christ and striving to live according to His teachings.

Contentment as a Counterbalance: Contentment, on the other hand, is the profound satisfaction and peace that emanates from recognising and appreciating the blessings we've received from God. It's the antidote to the restlessness that can arise from constant comparison and the pursuit of external achievements. Contentment doesn't mean we become complacent; rather, it implies a state of inner fulfilment and tranquillity that transcends external circumstances. Due to its importance, we will further cover this great virtue in chapter 26.

The Synergy of Godliness and Contentment: The synergy between godliness and contentment is profound. When we focus on cultivating a godly character, our priorities shift. Our hearts become attuned to God's will, and we begin to treasure the eternal over the temporary. As our relationship with God deepens, we realise that He is the ultimate source of joy, peace, and security, not the world's fleeting pleasures.

In this context, contentment isn't a passive resignation to circumstances; instead, it's an active choice to embrace God's providence and trust in His wisdom. When godliness and contentment coexist, we find ourselves less prone to the pitfalls of comparison, envy, and greed. Instead of constantly chasing after more, we learn to appreciate the sufficiency of what we have and acknowledge that our true worth is derived from our relationship with God.

The Great Gain: The verse highlights that these synergies—this harmonious blend of godliness and contentment—is indeed "great gain." It's a treasure that enriches the soul, grants us a clearer perspective on life's purpose, and leads to a deeper sense of fulfilment. This gain often stands apart in a world that measures success by material standards. It's an enrichment of the spirit, a treasure that grows over time, and a legacy that transcends earthly achievements.

In pursuing godliness, we discover contentment; in embracing contentment, we draw closer to godliness. This synergy shapes us into individuals who find contentment not in fleeting comparisons or material abundance but in God's unchanging and boundless love. As we walk this path, we bear witness to a life that reflects the beauty of God's design—a life where godliness and contentment intertwine to create a legacy of true and lasting gain.

God's Provision: *"And my God shall supply all your need according to His riches in glory by Christ Jesus"* (Philippians 4:19). Philippians reassures us of God's provision. While pursuing wealth is not inherently wrong, it should never overshadow our reliance on God's abundant provision for our needs.

The Parable of the Rich Fool: The Parable of the Rich Fool, found in Luke 12:16-21, is a poignant and powerful story that serves as a cautionary tale about the dangers of placing excessive emphasis on material wealth while neglecting the Kingdom of God and spiritual priorities.

The Rich Man's Perspective: In the parable, our Lord Jesus presents the story of a rich man whose land yields an abundant harvest. Faced with this windfall, the rich man's immediate reaction is to consider how he can store up his newfound wealth for himself. He envisions building larger barns to hoard his surplus crops, seemingly believing that his accumulated possessions will secure his future and bring him lasting satisfaction.

The Illusion of Security: The rich man's actions and mindset reflect a common human tendency—to seek security and contentment in earthly possessions. His focus on material accumulation blinds him to life's transient nature and future uncertainties. He falsely believes that his wealth can provide ultimate security and fulfilment, unaware that his time on Earth is limited.

Spiritual Bankruptcy: Tragically, the rich man's preoccupation with material wealth leads to spiritual impoverishment. God's response to him is a sobering reminder that the abundance of possessions doesn't measure life's value. Just as the man's physical life is abruptly cut short, his soul faces the consequence of misplaced priorities. Jesus illustrates the futility of investing solely in worldly treasures, which cannot save us from the deeper spiritual realities.

The Heart of the Lesson: The core lesson of this parable lies in its contrast between earthly wealth and spiritual wealth. The rich man's story is a stark reminder that wealth, when pursued at the expense of our relationship with God and our fellow human beings, leads to a hollow existence. The parable underscores the need to align our pursuits with God's kingdom values—to seek His righteousness first and to invest in treasures that have eternal significance.

Aligning with God's Priorities: By sharing this parable, our Lord Jesus urges us to evaluate our own lives and the values that drive our decisions. He challenges us to consider whether our focus is primarily on worldly gain or cultivating a rich heart toward God. This doesn't mean that wealth is inherently evil, but rather that it should be viewed and utilised in the context of God's purposes and priorities.

The True Treasure: The rich man's tragic fate reminds us that the true treasure lies not in material accumulation but in an intimate relationship with God. When our pursuit of wealth is guided by love for God and compassion for others, it becomes a means to further God's work, bless others, and glorify His name.

In a world that often glorifies material success and accumulation, the Parable of the Rich Fool is a vital reminder to examine our hearts, prioritise our pursuits, and ensure that our wealth aligns with God's purposes. It teaches us to value spiritual wealth, which enriches our lives here on Earth and our eternal destiny.

Generosity and Stewardship: *"Command those who are rich in this present age not to be haughty, nor to trust in uncertain riches but in the living God, who gives us richly all things to enjoy"* (1 Timothy 6:17).

The verse emphasises the call for those with wealth to be generous and to recognise that their riches are a gift from God. Viewing wealth as a tool for stewardship and service allows us to maintain a healthy perspective.

St. John Chrysostom, a revered early church father, wrote, *"Not to enable the poor to share in our goods is to steal from them and deprive them of life. The goods we possess are not ours, but theirs."* Chrysostom's words remind us that our pursuit of wealth should include a commitment to share with those in need.

Contentment and Eternal Treasure: *"Do not lay up for yourselves treasures on earth, where moth and rust destroy and where thieves break in and steal; but lay up for yourselves treasures in heaven, where neither moth nor rust destroys and where thieves do not break in and steal"* (Matthew 6:19-20).

St Matthew's words remind us of the impermanence of earthly wealth. Pursuing wealth without regard for eternal treasures can lead to spiritual emptiness. Our focus should be on storing treasures in heaven through righteous living and acts of kindness.

Pursuing wealth is not inherently wrong, but Christian principles must cautiously guide it. By acknowledging God's provision, learning from the parable of the rich fool, practising generosity and stewardship, drawing wisdom from early church fathers like St. John Chrysostom, reflecting on a story from the Coptic Church, and seeking eternal treasures, we can navigate the pursuit of wealth while keeping our faith central. This balanced approach ensures that our pursuit of wealth aligns with the values of our Christian journey.

The challenge of pursuing wealth while maintaining Christian values is a pertinent issue in today's materialistic world. Young Christian families often grapple with the tension between financial ambitions and spiritual priorities. Addressing this challenge involves fostering a balanced perspective on wealth, stewardship, and contentment in light of Christian teachings.

Understanding the Challenge:

Pursuing wealth can become a stumbling block when it takes precedence over spiritual growth, relationships, and acts of service. It can lead to misplaced priorities, materialism, and a neglect of the core values that guide Christian families.

Impact on Faith and Relationships:

The challenge of pursuing wealth can have profound effects on young Christian families:

- **Spiritual Erosion:** An obsessive focus on wealth accumulation can erode spiritual growth, pushing aside prayer, worship, and time spent in fellowship with God.

- **Strained Relationships:** Pursuing wealth can lead to an imbalance between work and family life, causing strain on marital and familial relationships.
- **Comparison and Envy:** Comparing one's financial status with others can lead to feelings of envy, discontentment, and a loss of focus on the blessings God has provided.

Addressing the Challenge:

Young Christian family needs to learn how to approach the pursuit of wealth in a way that aligns with Christian values:

- **Stewardship Mentality:** Families need to learn how to adopt and acquire a stewardship mentality, recognising that wealth is a blessing from God. Encourage them to manage their resources responsibly and generously, recognising their role as caretakers of God's gifts.
- **Seek First the Kingdom:** Remind yourself of our Lord Jesus' teaching to seek first the Kingdom of God and His righteousness. Emphasise that focusing on spiritual growth and building godly character should precede material pursuits.
- **Contentment:** Discuss the importance of contentment, regardless of financial circumstances. Help your family to recognise that true fulfilment comes from a deep relationship with God rather than material possessions.
- **Work-Life Balance:** Encourage each other to strike a healthy work-life balance. Prioritise quality time with family, personal well-being, spiritual nourishment, and career aspirations.
- **Generosity:** Highlight the significance of giving back to the needy and the weaker members of the body of

Christ, the community, and those in need. Teach your family to embrace a lifestyle of generosity, using your resources to bless others as an expression of their faith. Practice generosity beyond the tithes.

- **Financial Planning:** Practice wise financial planning, including saving, investing, and budgeting. Help families set financial goals that align with their values and long-term priorities.
- **Prayerful Decision-Making:** Encourage each other to seek God's guidance in financial decisions, praying for discernment and wisdom. Instil a sense of responsibility to make choices that honour God's principles.

The challenge of pursuing wealth while maintaining Christian values is complex, but it can be navigated with a heart committed to stewardship, contentment, and faith-driven decisions. By placing spiritual growth and God's Kingdom at the forefront, young Christian families can pursue financial goals in alignment with their faith, ensuring that their pursuit of wealth contributes to the betterment of themselves, their families, and the broader community.

In aligning our financial endeavours with Christian principles, we have explored the path of pursuing wealth with integrity, stewardship, and a heart focused on eternal treasures. As we conclude this chapter, we embark on a new journey that delves into the intricate tapestry of technology in our lives. In Chapter 18, 'Navigating a Technological World with Christian Wisdom,' we will navigate the dynamic landscape of digital innovations and virtual connections, seeking to uphold our Christian values while embracing the opportunities and challenges of this digital age. Just as we've strived to approach wealth with wisdom, let us now embark on a quest to navigate the seas of technology, permanently anchored by our faith, and guided by the light of Christ.

Chapter 18

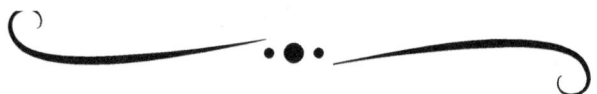

Navigating a Technological World with Christian Wisdom

In the tapestry of our lives, technology has emerged as a vibrant thread, intricately weaving itself into the fabric of our daily existence. Technology is an ever-present companion from the moment we wake to the sound of an alarm on our smartphones to the hours spent engaged in digital tasks and the moments shared with friends and loved ones through virtual platforms. It promises efficiency, connection, and information at our fingertips, offering a tapestry of convenience and innovation.

Yet, within this intricate web of technological advancements lie opportunities and challenges that demand our attention. The digital age has ushered in unprecedented connectivity levels, reshaping how we communicate, work, and even worship. However, as we embrace the allure of screens and algorithms, we must also recognise the delicate balance required to navigate this technological world with Christian wisdom.

In this chapter, we go deeper into the profound implications of living in a digital era marked by rapid technological evolution. We explore how technology influences our spiritual journey, challenges our relationships, and tests the boundaries of our faith. As we journey through the digital landscape, we seek to discern the paths that lead us closer to God's heart, even amidst the digital noise.

The convergence of technology and spirituality presents both a call and a caution.

- How do we remain rooted in our Christian values while surfing the waves of digital innovation?
- How do we prioritise real-life connections in an age of virtual interactions?
- How do we discern the digital tools that can enhance our faith journey and those that may hinder it?

As we venture through this chapter, we seek Christian wisdom in the digital age. With a foundation of faith and a heart open to learning, we seek to navigate the sea of information, harness the power of technology for good, and safeguard our souls from the pitfalls that may lurk within the digital landscape. Together, we explore how we can engage with technology as faithful stewards, using it to enhance our spiritual growth, deepen our relationships, and ultimately draw nearer to the source of all wisdom—our Creator.

The Primacy of Relationships: *"So then, my beloved brethren, let every man be swift to hear, slow to speak, slow to wrath"* (James 1:19).

St. James encourages us to prioritise relationships over technology. Being attentive listeners, measured speakers, and slow to anger fosters healthier online and offline interactions.

The Tower of Babel: The story of the Tower of Babel (Genesis 11:1-9) warns against technological pursuits driven by arrogance. As technology enables us to communicate globally, we must remember to use it humbly and for constructive purposes.

Guarding the Heart: *"Keep your heart with all diligence, for out of it spring the issues of life"* (Proverbs 4:23).

Proverbs teaches us to safeguard our hearts, as technology's influence can shape our thoughts and emotions. Maintaining a Christ-centred heart helps us navigate technology's potential pitfalls.

Bishop Moussa, a visionary leader in the Coptic Church, once said, *"Let our use of technology reflect our commitment to Christ. Just as Christ used parables to teach truth, let us use our technological tools to spread love and truth in a world thirsty for both."** His words remind us that technology can be a tool for sharing the Gospel and embodying Christian virtues.

Detoxifying from Distractions: *"And whoever does not bear his cross and come after Me cannot be My disciple"* (Luke 14:27).

St Luke's words remind us to prioritise our relationship with Christ over technological distractions. Carving out intentional time for prayer and reflection detaches us from the constant digital buzz.

Setting Boundaries: *"And He said to them, "Come aside by yourselves to a deserted place and rest a while." For there were many coming and going, and they did not even have time to eat"* (Mark 6:31).

Even our Lord and Saviour Jesus recognised the importance of setting boundaries. Amid technological noise, we must find moments of rest and solitude to nurture our souls.

Navigating a technological world with Christian wisdom requires intentionality. By valuing relationships, humbly wielding technology, guarding our hearts, reflecting on the wisdom of Bishop Moussa, learning from the Christian story of two neighbours, detoxifying from distractions, and setting boundaries, we can harness technology's benefits while preserving our spiritual well-being. In doing so, we embody the teachings of Christ in the digital age and lead lives of purposeful connection and meaningful faith.

The challenge of living in a world saturated with technology is a prominent issue for young Christian families. The pervasive influence of digital devices, social media, and online platforms presents both opportunities and challenges. Addressing this issue involves cultivating a balanced and intentional approach to technology use while upholding Christian values.

Understanding the Challenge:

Technology has transformed how we live, communicate, and interact with the world. While it offers convenience and connection, it also poses challenges such as digital distractions, potential addiction, and exposure to content that may contradict Christian principles.

Impact on Faith and Relationships:

The challenge of technology's ubiquity can impact young Christian families in several ways:
- **Diminished Presence:** Constant connectivity to devices can lead to a diminished presence in real-life interactions, impacting the quality of relationships within the family.
- **Spiritual Neglect:** Excessive screen time can divert attention from spiritual practices such as prayer, Scripture reading, and worship, leading to a weakening of faith.

- **Exposure to Influences:** Unfiltered access to online content can expose children and teens to ideologies and values contradicting Christian teachings, necessitating intentional guidance.

Addressing the Challenge:

Guide young Christian family members on navigating the challenge of technology with wisdom and intentionality:
- **Establish Healthy Boundaries:** Encourage family members to set clear technological boundaries. Designate device-free times, such as during meals and family gatherings, to foster meaningful interactions.
- **Model Balanced Behaviour:** Lead by example. Demonstrate balanced technology use by limiting screen time, engaging in face-to-face conversations, and prioritising offline activities.
- **Prioritise Relationships:** Emphasise the importance of nurturing relationships within the family. Suggest family activities, outings, and shared hobbies that promote quality time and bonding.
- **Digital Discernment:** Teach children critical thinking skills to assess online content through a lens of Christian values. Encourage open discussions about what they encounter online.
- **Tech-Free Spaces:** Designate specific areas of the home, such as bedrooms, as technology-free zones to promote restful sleep and minimise digital distractions.
- **Cultivate Spiritual Practices:** Encourage the incorporation of technology in ways that enhance spiritual growth. Utilise online devotionals, podcasts, or Bible study apps to reinforce faith practices.

- **Educate on Online Etiquette:** Discuss the importance of respectful and ethical online behaviour. Teach children to use technology responsibly and avoid engaging in cyberbullying or harmful activities.
- **Digital Detox:** Recommend periodic digital detoxes, where the family disconnects from screens and engages in nature, art, or other offline activities that foster the challenge of living in a technology-driven world and call for intentional and balanced approaches from young Christian families. By incorporating technology thoughtfully, setting healthy boundaries, and nurturing authentic relationships, families can harness the benefits of technology while safeguarding their faith, values, and connections. This approach allows them to navigate the digital landscape with Christian wisdom and ensure that technology enhances, rather than hinders, their family life and spiritual journey.

Let me end this chapter with this beautiful, true story. In a bustling city, a young family was caught in the whirlwind of modern life. Both parents held demanding jobs, and their two children were engrossed in their own digital devices, often spending hours on social media and online games. While the family was well-connected through technology, they felt a growing distance in their real-life interactions.

Recognising the need for a change, the parents decided to embark on a unique experiment. They declared every Sunday to be a "Tech-Free Family Day." These days, all electronic devices are put away, and the family engages in activities that foster genuine connections and quality time together.

At first, the transition was challenging. The children resisted being disconnected from their screens, and the parents found it difficult to break away from work-related emails and notifications. However, as the weeks went by, something remarkable began to happen.

Navigating a Technological World with Christian Wisdom

On Tech-Free Family Days, the family rediscovered the joy of face-to-face conversations. They engaged in outdoor adventures, creative projects, and shared meals without the distractions of screens. The parents noticed that their children's communication skills improved, and they became more present and attentive to one another.

As they gathered around the dining table one Sunday, the parents shared their thoughts on the experience. The father reflected on how easily technology had taken away precious moments that could have been spent nurturing relationships. The mother spoke about the peace they found in intentionally disconnecting from the digital world, allowing their souls to breathe and rejuvenate.

Over time, the family found that this intentional practice strengthened their bonds and deepened their faith. They used the time to read Scripture together, pray as a family, and discuss spiritual topics. This simple yet powerful change in their routine allowed them to align their technological engagement with their Christian values.

The family's Tech-Free Family Days became a cherished tradition, reminding them that while technology has benefits, it's crucial to strike a balance that nurtures the soul and fosters genuine connections. Their story inspires others to navigate the technological world with Christian wisdom—using technology as a tool that enhances relationships and spirituality rather than one that hinders them.

In the modern world, technology has become an inseparable part of our lives, offering both convenience and challenges. The chapter delves into the intricate relationship between faith and technology, highlighting the need for Christian wisdom in navigating this digital era. The impact of technology on relationships, spirituality, and values is explored, emphasising the importance of finding balance and intentionality.

As technology continues to shape our lives, the call to navigate its influence with Christian wisdom is crucial. Striking a balance between digital engagement and real-life connections is a challenge that young Christian families face today. Families can cultivate a harmonious relationship with technology by setting healthy boundaries, modelling balanced behaviour, prioritising relationships, promoting digital discernment, fostering spiritual practices, and occasionally detoxifying from screens. The true story of a family's journey towards tech-free days demonstrates the transformative power of intentional digital engagement. By approaching technology as a tool that aligns with their Christian values and enriches their relationships and faith, families can embrace the benefits of the digital age without compromising their beliefs.

As we reflect on the intricate dance of faith and technology, we are reminded of the enduring foundation upon which our beliefs rest. In a world where the sands of culture and trends constantly shift, the need to anchor and amplify our Christian faith becomes all the more essential. Just as a lighthouse stands firm against the crashing waves, our faith provides a steady beacon amidst the turbulent currents of modernity.

Chapter 19: "Anchoring and Amplifying Christian Faith in a World of Shifting Sands," delves into the transformative power of unwavering faith and its capacity to shape our responses to the ever-evolving world around us. In a culture that often prizes transitory pleasures and fleeting ideologies, we explore the timeless truths that ground us in a purposeful existence.

Guided by scripture, wisdom from the early church fathers, and real-life insights, this chapter invites us to fortify our spiritual foundation. Through the lens of faith, we will navigate the complexities of morality, ethics, and social engagement, uncovering the practical applications of our beliefs in an ever-changing landscape.

Join us as we embark on a journey that seeks to anchor our faith in the unchanging love of Christ while amplifying its impact in a world where the tides of change are constant. Chapter 19 awaits, offering a roadmap for embracing the eternal truths that enable us to stand firm amidst the shifting sands of our time.

Chapter 19

Anchoring and Amplifying Christian Faith in a World of Shifting Sands

In an ever-evolving world, where cultural shifts and societal changes seem to rearrange the very foundations of our lives, the call to hold steadfast to our Christian faith resonates with newfound urgency. As followers of Christ, "Your faith is your address and identity" encapsulates the profound connection between one's beliefs and their sense of belonging and self. Let's delve into this idea further:

Faith as Your Address: In a world full of physical addresses, each representing a specific location, faith offers a unique address – a spiritual dwelling place where your heart finds its home. Just as a physical address gives you a sense of place in the world, your faith provides a profound sense of belonging to something greater than yourself. It becomes the space where your soul resides, you commune with the divine, and you draw strength and guidance. This address isn't limited by geography; it transcends boundaries, cultures, and languages. It's a place where you can find solace, purpose, and direction, regardless of your physical location.

Faith as Your Identity: Identity is more than just a name or appearance; it's the essence of who you are. Your faith shapes and moulds your identity in profound ways. It influences your values, priorities, and perspectives. Just as a physical address reflects a particular neighbourhood, your faith marks you as part of a spiritual community with shared beliefs and values. It's not just about what you believe but how those beliefs manifest in your actions and interactions. Your faith informs your choices, relationships, and how you navigate the world. A core part of your identity becomes evident in how you love, serve, and engage with others.

The Intersection of Address and Identity: Your faith is where your spiritual address and identity meet. It's where you find meaning and purpose and discover your true self in the context of your beliefs. Just as a physical address can shape your interactions with neighbours and your environment, your faith shapes how you interact with the world and the people around you. It's the lens through which you view life's challenges and joys and the compass that guides you through the complexities of existence.

Ultimately, "Your faith is your address and identity" speaks to the idea that your beliefs provide you with a sense of belonging, purpose, and direction. It's a reminder that while the world may change and circumstances may shift, your faith remains a constant anchor, shaping your journey and defining who you are at your core.

Let me start this significant chapter with the story of the Martyrs of Libya:

In recent history, the tragic events in Libya stand as a poignant testament to the indomitable faith of Coptic Christians. This gripping account illustrates the unyielding commitment of Egyptian Copts who stood unwaveringly in their faith in the face of unspeakable persecution and imminent death, becoming modern-day martyrs.

Amid the shifting sands of Libya's complex political landscape, a group of simple Egyptian Copts young men who left their country, families, wives, and children and went to work as terrorists targeted simple labourers looking for more resourceful means of living. In their darkest hours, these faithful individuals clung to their faith with unwavering determination, embodying the spirit of Christ's teachings even in the face of dire adversity.

Separated from their homes and families, these brave souls exhibited a resilience that transcends comprehension. Their faith remained unshaken in the shadow of death, serving as a beacon of inspiration for all who witnessed their ordeal.

Bound together by bonds forged through shared faith, these martyrs clung to prayer as their refuge and strength. Even as the threat of death loomed, their prayers reverberated with hope, forgiveness, and an unbreakable connection to God. Their spiritual resolve was a testament to the enduring power of faith, proving that even the darkest circumstances cannot extinguish the light of Christ within the hearts of His followers.

In their final moments, facing their persecutors with remarkable courage, these martyrs showed no fear. Instead, they invoked the teachings of Christ to forgive those who sought to harm them. Their act of forgiveness echoed Christ's own words on the cross, and their steadfastness in the face of violence revealed the transformative power of faith.

The sacrifice of these modern-day martyrs resonates deeply within the Coptic community and beyond. Their unwavering commitment to their faith and willingness to embrace the ultimate sacrifice in the name of Christ stand as a poignant reminder that even in a world that often seems hostile to religious beliefs, the light of faith can shine brightest in the darkest hours.

As we reflect on the story of the Martyrs of Libya, we are called to uphold the same steadfast faith in our lives. Their legacy serves as a rallying cry for all Coptic Christians, urging us to stand firm in our beliefs, to remain united as a community, and to be beacons of light in a world that often seeks to extinguish the flame of faith. Just as these martyrs found strength in their darkest moments, we too can draw inspiration from their example to navigate the complexities of the changing world with unwavering faith and unshakeable courage.

Faith Anchored in God's Word: *"So then faith comes by hearing, and hearing by the word of God"* (Romans 10:17). Saint Paul's epistle to the Romans underscores the foundational role of God's Word in shaping our faith. Our unwavering faith remains rooted in Scripture's timeless truths as the world changes.

The Story of Noah: The story of Noah (Genesis 6-9) illustrates the necessity of holding onto faith amidst changing circumstances. Amid a world of corruption, Noah's steadfast obedience to God's instructions preserved humanity's future.

Living Epistles of Christ: *"You are our epistle written in our hearts, known and read by all men"* (2 Corinthians 3:2). St. Paul's words remind us that our lives are open letters proclaiming our faith to the world. Our actions, attitudes, and love mirror Christ's teachings as the world transforms.

Early Church Wisdom: St. Clement of Alexandria, an esteemed early church father, once said, *"The true beauty of man is found in the image of God that he bears, which reflects the divine wisdom, the divine righteousness, and the divine holiness."* His words remind us that our faith shines most brightly when we embody the divine attributes of love, wisdom, and righteousness.

Boldness and Resilience: *"For God has not given us a spirit of fear, but of power and of love and of a sound mind"* (2 Timothy 1:7). The verse encourages us to embrace boldness and resilience in sharing our faith. Our unwavering message of hope and salvation remains constant as the world evolves.

The Conversion of Saint Paul: The story of St. Paul's conversion (Acts 9) illustrates the transformative power of encountering Christ. Personal encounters with Jesus continue to shape lives and fuel faith in a changing world.

Bearing Fruit through Seasons: *"And he shall be like a tree planted by the rivers of water, that brings forth its fruit in its season; his leaf also shall not wither; and whatever he does shall prosper"* (Psalm 1:3). Psalm 1 draws a parallel between a faithful life and a fruitful tree. Just as trees adapt through seasons, our faith thrives as we remain connected to the source—Christ.

Our Christian faith remains steadfast and unchanging as the world shifts and evolves. By anchoring our faith in God's Word, learning from biblical stories like Noah and the parable of the Sower, embodying Christ's teachings as living epistles, reflecting on the wisdom of early church fathers like St. Clement of Alexandria, drawing inspiration from the Coptic martyrs in Libya, embracing boldness through Paul's example, experiencing personal encounters with Christ, and remaining fruitful like a well-rooted tree, we navigate the changing world with unwavering faith. Our journey of embracing and sharing our faith is a testament to the enduring light of the Gospel, illuminating a changing world with the love and truth of Christ.

The challenge of living out and spreading the Christian faith is a central concern for young families in today's diverse and evolving society. As they strive to be faithful examples of Christ's teachings, they face the responsibility of nurturing their faith, passing it on to the next generation and positively impacting their communities.

Understanding the Challenge:

In a world marked by many beliefs, ideologies, and worldviews, young Christian families often navigate uncharted territory as they seek to live and share their faith authentically. This challenge can be both rewarding and daunting as they encounter diverse perspectives and changing cultural norms.

Impact on Faith and Relationships:

The challenge of living and spreading the Christian faith can impact young families in various ways:

- **Cultural Contrasts:** Families may encounter beliefs and practices that contradict their Christian values, prompting questions about how to engage respectfully without compromising their convictions.
- **Generational Transfer:** Passing on a vibrant and relevant faith to their children can be challenging, especially when cultural shifts and technological advances affect how young people perceive and experience spirituality.
- **Social Engagement:** As they strive to be salt and light in the world, families may face scepticism or opposition when expressing their faith in public or digital spaces.

Addressing the Challenge:

Guide young Christian family members in navigating the challenge of living and sharing their faith in a changing world:

- **Foundation of Knowledge:** Encourage your family to deepen their understanding of Christianity's

foundational teachings and how to apply them to contemporary situations. Equip them to address challenging questions with wisdom and humility.
- **Authenticity:** Emphasise the importance of authentic living. Encourage your family to align their actions with their beliefs, demonstrating Christ's love and compassion in their interactions with others.
- **Family Discipleship:** Empower each other to intentionally disciple your children through regular Bible study, prayer, and conversations about faith. Create opportunities for open dialogue where questions and doubts can be addressed openly.
- **Service and Outreach:** Encourage and support each other to actively engage in the church community and beyond your communities through acts of service and kindness. Whether through volunteering, supporting local initiatives, or being a source of encouragement, they can tangibly demonstrate Christ's love.
- **Digital Witness:** Discuss among family members and friends how families can leverage digital platforms to share their faith responsibly and positively. Offer guidance on using social media to spread uplifting messages, engage in discussions, and share personal testimonies.
- **Cultural Sensitivity:** Provide tools for navigating conversations with individuals of diverse backgrounds and beliefs. Teach families to approach discussions with empathy, respect, and a willingness to listen.
- **Small Group Engagement:** Recommend involvement in small groups or Bible studies within your church community. These spaces foster deeper relationships and provide opportunities for mutual growth and support.

In a world marked by constant change and diverse beliefs, young Christian families face the challenge of living and sharing their faith authentically. The impact on faith, relationships, and societal engagement is significant, prompting the need for guidance and strategies. Encouraging a strong foundation of knowledge, authenticity in living out beliefs, intentional family discipleship, active service and outreach, responsible digital witness, cultural sensitivity, and engagement in supportive small groups can equip young families to navigate this challenge effectively.

Living and sharing the Christian faith in a world of shifting sands is a noble endeavour that requires intentionality and resilience. Young Christian families have a vital role in shaping the future of their faith and positively impacting their communities. By anchoring themselves in the teachings of Christ, remaining authentic in their actions, nurturing faith within their families, extending love through service, wisely engaging in the digital realm, respecting diverse perspectives, and finding strength in community, they can navigate this challenge with grace and purpose. As they embrace the call to be Christ's witnesses in a changing world, they contribute to a legacy of faith that transcends generations and illuminates the path for others seeking the truth.

As we conclude our exploration of anchoring and amplifying our Christian faith, our journey leads us to the heart of the family—a sanctuary where faith takes root, flourishes, and shapes the lives of its members. Just as a garden requires nurturing and care to thrive, so too does the Christian family need intentional cultivation to stand strong in today's world.

Chapter 20: "Nurturing a Strong Christian Family in Today's World" invites us to delve into families' vital role in passing down the torch of faith from one generation to the next. In a society marked by rapid changes and shifting values, the family is a cornerstone of stability and a vessel for transmitting timeless principles.

Anchoring and Amplifying Christian Faith in a World of Shifting Sands

Drawing inspiration from biblical teachings, insights from wise spiritual leaders, and the experiences of real families, this chapter is a guidebook for cultivating a family culture deeply rooted in Christian values. We will explore the practical steps and intentional practices that foster spiritual growth, open communication, and enduring love within the family unit.

Join us as we embark on a journey that underscores the significance of family in shaping our spiritual foundations and navigating the challenges of contemporary life. Chapter 20 awaits, ready to equip us with the tools, wisdom, and inspiration needed to nurture a strong Christian family in today's world. This legacy will echo through generations to come.

Chapter 20

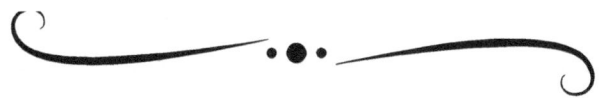

Nurturing a Strong Christian Family in Today's World

Amid the complexities of today's world, nurturing a strong Christian family is a sacred responsibility that resonates deeply within the hearts of Christian believers. Nurturing a strong Christian family today is challenging and crucial due to the profound shifts and complexities that modern society presents. The convergence of technological advancements, shifting cultural values, and changing family dynamics has created a unique set of challenges that can undermine the foundation of a Christian family. This makes nurturing a strong Christian family more vital than ever.

Build on the Rock: Reflecting on the teachings of our Lord Jesus Christ, the parable of the wise man who built his house on the rock (Matthew 7:24-27) captures the essence of nurturing a strong Christian family. Just as the wise man's house stood unwavering against the storms due to its foundation, so too shall our families endure life's trials when founded on Christ's unwavering principles.

Foundation in Love: *"And now abide faith, hope, love, these three; but the greatest of these is love"* (1 Corinthians 13:13). The verse teaches that love is the cornerstone of strong families. In the Coptic tradition, love is the bond that connects families, echoing the heart of Christ's teachings.

Foundation of Faith: The Legacy of Abraham's Family: The narrative of Abraham's familial journey (Genesis 12-25) holds a profound place in the annals of Coptic tradition. Abraham's unyielding faith in God was the adhesive that held his family together, establishing their legacy as paragons of unwavering faith.

Foundation of Christian Parenting with Purpose: *"And you, fathers, do not provoke your children to wrath, but bring them up in the training and admonition of the Lord"* (Ephesians 6:4). Ephesians offers guidance for parenting in the Coptic spirit. Fostering spiritual growth in children aligns with the values cherished by our Coptic forefathers.

Foundation of Christian Mutual Respect: Mutual respect within a Christian family creates an environment where love, trust, and cooperation flourish. It reflects the beauty of Christ's teachings and serves as a powerful witness to the world. As family members honour and value, one another as cherished creations of God, they contribute to building a strong and Christ-centred household where individuals grow in faith and love together. How can we foster this character in our marriage?

1. **Imitating Christ's Humility:** Philippians 2:3-4 – "Let nothing be done through selfish ambition or conceit, but in lowliness of mind let each esteem others better than himself. Let each of you look out not only for his own interests, but also for the interests of others."

2. **Listening and Understanding:** James 1:19 – "So then, my beloved brethren, let every man be swift to hear, slow to speak, slow to wrath."
3. **Open Communication:** Ephesians 4:29 – "Let no corrupt word proceed out of your mouth, but what is good for necessary edification, that it may impart grace to the hearers."
4. **Valuing Each Other's Dignity:** 1 Peter 2:17 – "Honor all people. Love the brotherhood. Fear God. Honor the king."
5. **Servant Leadership:** Ephesians 5:25 – "Husbands, love your wives, just as Christ also loved the church and gave Himself for her."
6. **Resolving Conflict:** Colossians 3:13 – "bearing with one another, and forgiving one another, if anyone has a complaint against another; even as Christ forgave you, so you also must do."
7. **Prayer and Unity:** Psalm 133:1- "Behold, how good and how pleasant it is for brethren to dwell together in unity!"

Dear reader, it is evident that this foundational aspect occupies the most significant space in our commentary due to its immeasurable and profound significance, particularly within the context of marriage.

The Parable of the Prodigal Son: The parable of the prodigal son (Luke 15:11-32) resonates with Coptic families, highlighting forgiveness and reconciliation. Love and forgiveness, upheld by Coptic teachings, can mend and renew relationships.

Learning from Other Families: Witnessing strong Christian families around the world inspires our Coptic families. Embracing shared prayers, family traditions, and open communication aligns with our Coptic heritage.

St. Athanasius, the Apostolic, said, *"The Word of God assumed our nature that we might become like Him and partake of the divine nature."* His wisdom reminds us of the transformative power of Christ's presence in our families.

Coptic Family Story:

In the heart of a quaint Coptic village in Upper Egypt, the inspiring narrative of the Mikhail family unfolds. The Mikhail family embody the timeless values of faith, unity, and love cherished within the Coptic tradition. Their story serves as a radiant example of a family deeply rooted in Christ, facing life's trials with unwavering strength.

A Humble Beginning: The journey of the Mikhail family began modestly. Like many Coptic families, they relied on the foundation of prayer and the Scriptures. Their home was a sanctuary of shared meals, laughter, and heartfelt conversations that illuminated the presence of Christ in their midst.

A Test of Faith: As life unfolded, the Mikhail family encountered challenges that tested their faith. Financial struggles and health setbacks cast shadows, but their unwavering trust in God's providence sustained them. Their prayers were filled with gratitude for the blessings they did have and petitions for strength during times of trial.

Unity amid Diversity: The village's Coptic community was marked by its diverse members, each with unique backgrounds and stories. The Mikhail family embraced this diversity, opening their home to fellow Copts and sharing their faith with those seeking solace. Their family gatherings became a haven where different voices joined in praise and worship.

Lessons of Love and Sacrifice: During a particularly trying time, the Mikhail family displayed their commitment to each other in a powerful way. Despite limited resources, they extended hospitality to a displaced family who had lost everything. Their selflessness illustrated the profound love that Christ teaches, inspiring not only their children but also the entire village.

Passing down the Torch: The Mikhail children grew up witnessing their parents' unwavering faith. As they faced the challenges of adolescence and adulthood, the lessons learned from their parents' example resonated deeply. The family's legacy of love, humility, and reliance on God's grace provided a sturdy foundation for the younger generation.

A Beacon of Light: The Mikhail's' story reached beyond their village. Their steadfast faith and commitment to one another drew the admiration and respect of neighbouring communities. As their family grew, they continued to open their doors to fellow Copts, sharing meals, stories, and, most importantly, the Gospel's message of hope.

Enduring Legacy: Through the Mikhail family, the village witnessed the transformative power of faith. Their story became a source of inspiration for families seeking to navigate the challenges of a changing world while remaining anchored in Christ. The legacy of the Mikhail family continues to shine as a beacon of light in the Coptic community, a testament to the enduring strength that comes from a family rooted in love, unity, and unwavering faith.

The Mikhail family's story encapsulates the essence of nurturing a strong Coptic Christian family. Their journey exemplifies the teachings of Christ, the principles of the Coptic tradition, and the power of unwavering faith in the face of challenges. By cherishing their story, Coptic families are encouraged to continue embracing the values that have defined their heritage for generations.

Navigating the challenges of modern life while nurturing a strong Coptic Christian family demands thoughtful consideration. Anchoring our families in love, drawing wisdom from the family of Abraham, parenting with purpose in line with Coptic teachings, learning from parables like the prodigal son, gaining insight from global Christian families, resonating with contemporary family testimonies, following a biblical model of leadership, embracing the wisdom of Coptic Church fathers, cherishing Coptic family stories, and trusting in God's guidance, we cultivate robust families that remain true to our Coptic heritage. By doing so, we honour our Coptic faith, creating a haven of love, faith, and unity amid the complexities of the changing world.

Maintaining a strong Christian family is a central challenge for young couples seeking to uphold their faith while navigating the complexities of modern life. The challenge involves creating a Christ-centred home environment, fostering healthy relationships, and passing on a legacy of faith to future generations. Remember, you're creating the next generation.

Understanding the Challenge:

In a world where secular influences, busy schedules, and cultural shifts abound, young Christian families face fortifying their bonds while remaining rooted in their faith. This challenge requires intentional efforts to prioritise spiritual growth, open communication, and genuine connection.

Impact on Family Dynamics:

The challenge of maintaining a strong Christian family can have far-reaching effects:

- **Spiritual Resilience:** Families may face spiritual battles that challenge their faith and unity. Pressures from outside influences can test their commitment to Christ-centred living.

- **Balancing Priorities:** Juggling work, family commitments, and personal pursuits can strain family time and hinder cultivating a spiritually nurturing environment.
- **Generational Impact:** The example set by parents significantly impacts their children's perception of faith and values. A strong Christian family can potentially shape future generations' spiritual trajectory.

Addresing the Challenge:

- **Prioritise Family Devotions:** Encourage each other to engage in regular times of prayer, Bible study, and worship together. These practices anchor the family in their shared faith journey.
- **Open Communication:** Foster an environment where open communication is valued. Parents should create spaces where children feel comfortable discussing their questions, doubts, and experiences.
- **Quality Time:** Urge families to prioritise quality time together. Whether through shared meals, outings, or engaging in hobbies, spending intentional time together strengthens family bonds.
- **Model Christ-likeness:** Lead by example in modelling Christ-like behaviour. Display love, forgiveness, humility, and servanthood in daily interactions, showcasing the fruits of a life lived for God.
- **Encourage Individual Growth:** Support each family member's personal spiritual growth. Encourage parents to help children explore their unique talents, passions,

and callings within the context of their faith.

- **Set Healthy Boundaries:** Discuss the importance of setting boundaries to protect family time, including designated times when technology is put aside to engage in meaningful interactions.
- **Create Family Traditions:** Encourage the establishment of family traditions that reinforce Christian values, such as volunteering as a family in church events or participating in community service.
- **Seek Accountability:** Emphasise the value of connecting with other families or mentors who share similar values. This sense of community offers support, encouragement, and accountability.

In the intricate tapestry of today's world, the challenge of nurturing a strong Christian family stands as a testament to the enduring power of faith, love, and unity. As the currents of modernity pull families in various directions, the call to anchor one's household in Christ's teachings remains resolute. The parable of the wise man and the rock serves as a timeless reminder that a strong Christian family stands firm against life's storms when built on the unshakable foundation of faith.

With love as the cornerstone and guided by the teachings of the Coptic tradition, families find inspiration in the stories of Abraham's faith, the prodigal son's reconciliation, and the exemplary witness of fellow Christian families. The wisdom of St. Athanasius underscores the transformative potential of integrating Christ's presence into the heart of the family.

The story of the Mikhail family illuminates the path to nurturing a strong Coptic Christian family. Through trials and triumphs, they exemplify the unwavering commitment to faith, unity, and hospitality—a legacy reverberating through generations and influencing communities far beyond their own.

Nurturing a Strong Christian Family in Today's World

Amidst the myriad challenges of contemporary life, nurturing a strong Coptic Christian family requires an intentional approach. By embracing the values of love, communication, togetherness, and Christ-like leadership, families can create a haven that shields against the world's storms. As each family embarks on this sacred journey, they contribute to the rich tapestry of the Coptic tradition, weaving threads of faith and unity that strengthen the entire community.

In the end, nurturing a strong Coptic Christian family is a profound testament to the power of faith in shaping lives, fortifying bonds, and illuminating the path toward Christ. With devotion and determination, Coptic families can rise above the challenges of the modern age, creating homes that radiate with the light of God's love and the strength of unwavering faith.

As we bid farewell to the insights of nurturing solid Christian families, our journey now directs our gaze toward a topic of profound significance—purity in Christian living for young families. Just as a foundation upholds the integrity of a structure, embracing purity safeguards the essence of family life and faith in a world that often challenges these values.

Chapter 21: "Embracing Purity in Christian Living for Young Families" explores the delicate interplay of purity, faith, and family dynamics. In a culture marked by shifting norms and prevalent influences, pursuing purity becomes both a steadfast commitment and a formidable challenge for young families.

With biblical wisdom, shared experiences, and practical guidance, this chapter delves into the essence of purity as a cornerstone of Christian living. We will navigate the nuanced landscape of maintaining moral clarity, upholding integrity, and fostering open dialogue within the family unit. The pervasive challenge of pornography will be addressed as it pertains to young families, with an unwavering commitment to preserving the sanctity of relationships, faith, and personal well-being.

Join us as we explore purity's profound significance in the context of young Christian families. Chapter 21 awaits, ready to illuminate the path toward embracing purity and nurturing a family life that radiates with the virtues of holiness, love, and unwavering faith.

Chapter 21

Embracing Purity in Christian Living for Young Families

In the journey of Christian living, purity holds a sacred and transformative significance. It calls us to cultivate a lifestyle that reflects holiness, integrity, and moral clarity. For young families navigating the complexities of today's world, embracing purity becomes both a guiding principle and a formidable challenge. In a society marked by shifting cultural norms, moral ambiguity, and an inundation of information, the pursuit of purity takes on a profound significance.

One particular challenge that young families often encounter on this path is the pervasive issue of pornography. The accessibility of explicit content in the digital age has created an environment where guarding against impurity requires heightened awareness and proactive measures. This chapter not only delves into the essence of purity in Christian living but also addresses the specific challenge of pornography, acknowledging its potential to erode the foundations of faith, relationships, and personal well-being.

As we embark on this exploration, we seek to uncover the beauty and depth of living a life marked by purity while addressing the practical steps and considerations that resonate with the unique dynamics of young family life. We will navigate the delicate balance between embracing the virtues of purity and safeguarding our families from the influences that threaten it, particularly the pervasive impact of pornography. Through open dialogue, scriptural insights, and shared experiences, we aim to equip young families with the tools and wisdom needed to navigate this aspect of purity in today's challenging world.

Purity in Heart and Mind: *"Purity is to will one thing,"* Pope Shenouda III's profound words echo the essence of our faith. In the context of Christian purity, this principle extends to aligning our desires and intentions with God's divine will. By nurturing purity within our hearts and minds, we create a fertile ground for a family life that resonates harmoniously with God's intentions.

Holiness in Marriage and the Sacrament of Matrimony: Purity within the sacred bond of marriage is illuminated by the teachings of Pope Shenouda III. His affirmation that *"your marriage can be holy and full of love"* underscores the profound holiness inherent in the sacrament of matrimony. The Coptic Orthodox Church views marriage as a holy sacrament, a union blessed by God that mirrors the relationship between Christ and His Church. This sacrament is celebrated with profound reverence, emphasising the sanctification of the couple's love through the grace of God.

The Sacrament of Matrimony in Coptic Orthodox Teaching: The sacrament of matrimony is central to the Coptic Orthodox tradition. Rooted in ancient apostolic practices, this sacrament is a divine institution where two individuals are united as one in the presence of God and His Church. The couple's love is sanctified through the sacrament, becoming an earthly reflection of the eternal love between Christ and His Church.

In the Coptic Orthodox Church, the sacrament of matrimony is a mystical union guided by sacred rituals, prayers, and blessings. The crowning ceremony, symbolic of the crowns of martyrdom, signifies the couple's commitment to selfless love and sacrifice within the holy bond of marriage, symbolising the selfless love of Christ to His church, who died for her and Saint Mary in her love, wisdom and humility representing the church. The exchange of rings represents the unbreakable unity between husband and wife.

The Role of the Holy Spirit: At the heart of the sacrament of matrimony is the presence and guidance of the Holy Spirit. Just as the Holy Spirit descended upon the apostles at Pentecost, He is invoked to descend upon the couple, blessing and sanctifying their union. The Holy Spirit empowers the couple to live out their marital vows with love, humility, and mutual respect. His divine presence infuses the sacrament with spiritual grace, uniting the couple in a bond that reflects Christ's love for His Church.

Spiritual Dimensions of Matrimony: The Coptic Orthodox Church greatly emphasises the spiritual dimensions of matrimony. The couple is called to be spiritual companions, supporting one another in their journey toward salvation. The sacrament encourages mutual respect, selflessness, and humility, fostering an environment where the love between spouses mirrors Christ's love for His Church.

Embracing Purity in Marriage: The principles of purity resonate deeply within the sacrament of matrimony. The couple is called to uphold the purity of their love, seeking God's grace to live in harmony and faithfulness. Even in the face of challenges, the vow to honour and cherish one another reflects the commitment to maintain the purity of their marital bond.

Pornography is a topic that raises significant concerns from a Christian perspective, invoking discussions about purity, moral values, and the teachings of the Bible. When examining pornography through the lens of the Christian faith, several reasons highlight its problematic nature:

1. **Distortion of God's Design:** Pornography often presents a distorted and twisted version of God's intended design for human sexuality. It objectifies individuals and reduces them to objects of lust, undermining the sacredness of the sexual union as designed by God.

"For this is the will of God, your sanctification: that you should abstain from sexual immorality; that each of you should know how to possess his own vessel in sanctification and honor..." (1 Thessalonians 4:3-4).

2. **Dignity of God's Creation:** Engaging with pornography contributes to the degradation of the inherent dignity of each individual, as people are made in the image of God. Such content often involves exploitation, harming the very essence of God's creation.

"So God created man in His own image; in the image of God He created him; male and female He created them" (Genesis 1:27).

3. **Erosion of Godly Relationships:** The distorted view of intimacy presented in pornography can distort perceptions of healthy relationships and diminish emotional and spiritual bonds between partners.

"Husbands, love your wives, just as Christ also loved the church and gave Himself for her..." (Ephesians 5:25).

4. **Addictive and Escalating Nature:** Pornography can be highly addictive due to its ability to stimulate the

brain's pleasure centres. This may lead to a dangerous cycle of addiction and the need for increasingly explicit content.

"All things are lawful for me, but I will not be brought under the power of any" (1 Corinthians 6:12).

5. **Spiritual and Moral Integrity:** Engaging in pornography contradicts the principles of sexual purity and moral values taught in the Bible. Such actions can lead to guilt, shame, and a sense of spiritual distance from God.

"Blessed are the pure in heart, for they shall see God" (Matthew 5:8).

6. **Impact on Self-Image:** The unrealistic and idealised portrayals of the human body in pornography can contribute to negative self-esteem and body image issues, especially among young people.

"Do you not know that your bodies are members of Christ?" (1 Corinthians 6:15).

7. **Promoting Exploitation:** The pornography industry is often linked to human trafficking, exploitation, and the perpetuation of harmful stereotypes. Consuming pornography indirectly supports these negative aspects.

"Let no one deceive you with empty words, for because of these things the wrath of God comes upon the sons of disobedience" (Ephesians 5:6).

8. **Cultural Impact:** Widespread consumption of pornography can contribute to a culture that normalises and glorifies sexual objectification, ultimately affecting societal attitudes and behaviours.

"And do not be conformed to this world, but be transformed by the renewing of your mind..." (Romans 12:2).

As followers of Christ, we must uphold the principles of purity, honour, and integrity in all aspects of our lives, including our thoughts and actions concerning human sexuality. The Bible offers guidance and wisdom to navigate these challenging issues while striving to live in alignment with God's divine plan for our lives.

Understanding the Challenge:

Pursuing a pure Christian life can be daunting in a culture that often glorifies instant gratification, individualism, and moral relativism. Young Christian families struggle to maintain integrity in thought, action, and relationships while standing firm in their commitment to biblical values.

Impact on Faith and Relationships:

The challenge of living a pure Christian life can have profound effects on young families:

- **Cultural Influences:** Families may encounter media, peer pressure, and societal norms that contradict Christian principles of purity, leading to feelings of isolation and tension.
- **Marital Intimacy:** The challenge of maintaining a pure Christian life extends to marital intimacy, where couples must navigate healthy boundaries and align their physical relationship with biblical teachings.
- **Parenting Values:** Young parents must instil values of purity in their children while addressing the potential exposure to explicit content and peer pressures at an increasingly young age.

Addressing the Challenge:

Guide your family in navigating the challenge of living a pure Christian life:

- **Cultivate Godly Character:** Encourage each other to cultivate Godly character traits such as self-discipline, self-control, humility, and a deep reverence for God's commandments.

- **Mind Renewal:** Embrace the importance of renewing the mind through continuous repentance, practising the great sacrament of repentance and confession, Scripture, and prayer. By saturating your thoughts with God's Word, families can better discern and reject influences that lead away from purity.

- **Boundaries in Relationships:** Discuss healthy boundaries in relationships, emphasising the importance of mutual respect and open communication. Teach children and teens about appropriate boundaries with friends and potential romantic interests.

- **Media Discernment:** Families should be equipped with tools to navigate media consumption critically. Encourage parents to be aware of their children's media exposure and guide them in making choices aligned with purity.

- **Honour in Marriage:** Address the significance of purity within marriage, helping couples align their physical intimacy with God's design for marriage. Discuss ways to communicate and grow together in this aspect of their relationship in the fear & love of God.

- **Parent-Child Communication:** Parents should encourage each other to create a safe space to discuss topics of purity with their children at age-appropriate levels under the guidance of the church's spiritual fathers. Provide resources and guidance on addressing challenging questions with grace and honesty.

- **Supportive Community:** Encourage family members to seek out a supportive Christian community where they can find encouragement, accountability, and mentorship in their pursuit of purity.
- **Prayer and Accountability:** Highlight the role of prayer in maintaining purity and suggest the value of confession fathers, spiritual father accountability partners or mentors who can provide guidance and support.

Focus on Christ: Above all, emphasise the centrality of Christ in the pursuit of purity. Families can navigate the world's challenges with unwavering faith and integrity by continually seeking His guidance, grace, and transformative power. In a world filled with shifting values and moral complexities, embracing purity in Christian living for young families is an essential calling. This chapter has explored the profound significance of purity within the context of faith and relationships, highlighting the unique challenges that families face, including the issue of pornography. Families can navigate these challenges with resilience and grace by anchoring themselves in the teachings of Scripture, the wisdom of church fathers, and the grace of God.

Pursuing purity is not merely a set of rules but a transformation journey. It requires intentional efforts to align hearts, minds, and actions with the principles of Christ's love and holiness. As families strive for purity, they create an environment where love, respect, and Godly values flourish. By upholding purity within marriages, fostering open communication, setting healthy boundaries, and seeking guidance from the church community, families can overcome the challenges posed by impurity and pornography.

In this pursuit, the love of Christ serves as a guiding light, illuminating the path toward a life marked by purity and holiness. As families embrace this journey together, they witness the transformative power of God's grace, setting an example for future generations. In the face of challenges, may the words of the apostle Paul resonate in our hearts:

"Finally, brethren, whatever things are true, whatever things are noble, whatever things are just, whatever things are pure, whatever things are lovely, whatever things are of good report, if there is any virtue and if there is anything praiseworthy—meditate on these things" (Philippians 4:8).

With hearts enlightened by the quest for purity, we transition to an equally vital virtue that shapes the fabric of young Christian families—unselfishness. Just as the dawn illuminates the world, unselfishness radiates a transformative light that dispels darkness and ushers in harmony within family dynamics.

In Chapter 22: "Embracing Unselfishness in Young Christian Families," we delve into the profound essence of putting others before ourselves—a principle that resonates deeply with the teachings of Christ. Within the intricate dance of family life, unselfishness paves the way for sacrificial love, mutual respect, and a shared journey toward spiritual growth.

Guided by scriptural insights, shared experiences, and the legacy of selflessness exemplified by the saints, this chapter embarks on a journey to explore how unselfishness nurtures resilient families. It offers practical wisdom on cultivating an environment of humility, considering the needs of others, and aligning familial aspirations with God's purpose.

As we explore unselfishness, we invite you to accompany us on a path that resonates with Christ's teachings of selfless love. Chapter 22 beckons—a chapter that seeks to illuminate the beauty of unselfishness as it intertwines with the tapestry of young Christian families.

Chapter 22

Embracing Unselfishness in Young Christian Families

Before my ordination as a priest within my great and amazing Coptic Orthodox Church, I had the privilege of encountering a remarkable Christian family. The husband, George and Karen, the blessed wife, both held teaching positions in the Catholic school system. However, their lives took an unexpected turn when the wife was diagnosed with the formidable disease known as multiple sclerosis. As time passed, her condition deteriorated to the point where she became confined to a wheelchair.

Despite their challenges, their devotion to each other and their faith shone brightly. The couple had beautiful children, and the husband stepped into the role of a true servant-leader for his family. Each day, after finishing his work at school, George would return home and wholeheartedly devote himself to his family's well-being. He tirelessly assisted his children with their homework, ensuring their academic success.

What truly exemplified his selflessness was the profound care he provided to his wife. Every day, without fail or any sign of complaint, he gently pushed her wheelchair around the neighbourhood. This act of love wasn't just a routine; it was a tangible expression of his dedication to providing her with the essentials for her well-being. Even as the sun set and the world around them grew quiet, he remained her steadfast companion.

Yet, his selflessness didn't stop there. He extended his service beyond the confines of his family's home. Inspired by his faith, he joined the Australian Corrective Service as a volunteer, offering his time to mentor inmates and give them hope. He even visited the infamous prisons in New South Wales, walking the halls to bring solace and guidance to those who had lost their way.

The unselfishness displayed by this man resonated deeply with me. Through his actions, he embodied the teachings of Christ and exemplified the essence of sacrificial love. His life mirrored the Saviour's selfless journey, and his commitment to his family and community reflected Christ's teachings of service and compassion. Everyone who has known or met him could easily see the amazing grace that radiated from his face.

In this man's life, I found a living example of unselfishness that closely resembled the character of Christ Himself. His humility, dedication, and love for his family and fellow humans showcased the beauty of living a life in alignment with Christian principles. He lived out the truth that genuine Christianity is not just a creed we profess but a life we embody—a life marked by actions that mirror the selflessness and love of our Saviour.

Amidst the resplendent tapestry of our Christian belief value system, one radiant thread stands out—the unselfish love personified by our Lord Jesus Christ. This section delves into the sacred principle of unselfishness, drawing wisdom from the selfless nature of Christ's sacrifice, the teachings of church fathers, the illuminating verses of the Bible, and the treasured stories of faith that guide us in the path of selflessness.

Selfishness can harm a marriage, causing strain, conflicts, and even the deterioration of the relationship deterioration over time. Here are some of the impacts of selfishness in a marriage:

1. **Communication Breakdown:** Selfishness often leads to poor communication. When one or both partners prioritise their own needs and desires without considering their spouse's feelings, communication can become one-sided and ineffective. This breakdown can create misunderstandings and lead to unresolved conflicts.

2. **Resentment and Anger:** Selfish behaviour can breed resentment and anger in the marriage. The partner who feels consistently overlooked or unvalued may develop feelings of bitterness, leading to emotional distance and strained interactions.

3. **Lack of Trust:** Selfishness erodes trust between partners. When one spouse consistently puts their own interests before the marriage, the other spouse may question their commitment to the relationship. This lack of trust can create an environment of insecurity and instability.

4. **Emotional Distance:** Selfishness can result in emotional distance between partners. When one partner's needs are consistently prioritised over the other's, the neglected partner may withdraw emotionally as a protective mechanism.

5. **Conflict Escalation:** Selfishness often leads to escalated conflicts. When one partner's self-centred behaviour clashes with the other's desires, disagreements can become heated and unproductive, potentially leading

to hurtful arguments.

6. **Diminished Intimacy:** Selfishness can negatively impact intimacy in a marriage. Emotional and physical intimacy thrives in an environment of mutual care and consideration. When selfishness takes centre stage, intimacy can wane, affecting both emotional and physical closeness.
7. **Neglect of Partnership:** Selfishness can cause a shift from a partnership to a one-sided relationship. A marriage is built on the idea of mutual support and shared responsibilities. When one partner becomes excessively selfish, the balance of the partnership is disrupted.
8. **Stagnant Growth:** Selfishness can hinder personal and relational growth. Partners may be less inclined to invest time and effort in the marriage if they feel their needs are not being met. This can result in a lack of personal and collective growth.
9. **Parenting Challenges:** Selfishness can impact parenting dynamics if children are part of the family. Disagreements over parenting styles and priorities can arise if partners are focused on their own desires rather than the well-being of the family unit.
10. **Marital Dissatisfaction:** Over time, unchecked selfishness can lead to overall marital dissatisfaction. The lack of emotional fulfilment, mutual respect, and shared goals can make partners feel unfulfilled and even contemplate separation or divorce.

Understanding selfishness: Selfishness can arise from a variety of factors, both internal and external. Understanding these underlying reasons can help couples navigate and address selfish behaviour within their marriage. Here are some common reasons why individuals may become selfish:

1. **Insecurity:** Insecurity can lead people to focus excessively on themselves to protect their emotional well-being. They may believe that they can avoid disappointment or rejection by putting their own needs first.
2. **Lack of Awareness:** Sometimes, individuals may not realise the extent of their selfish behaviour. Their own wants might consume them, and they may overlook the impact of their actions on their partner and the relationship.
3. **Unmet Needs:** When individuals feel their needs are consistently unmet, they may turn inward and prioritise themselves. This can be a response to feeling neglected or undervalued in the marriage.
4. **Cultural and Social Influences:** Cultural norms and societal pressures can also contribute to selfish behaviour. Self-centeredness may be more common in cultures that emphasise individualism as people prioritise personal success and happiness.
5. **Stress and Overwhelm:** When dealing with high stress levels, individuals may become more self-focused as a way to cope. The demands of work, family, and other responsibilities can lead to a self-centred mindset.
6. **Lack of Communication Skills:** People who struggle with effective communication may resort to selfish behaviour to assert their needs or desires. They may not know how to express themselves healthier and more considerate.
7. **Past Experiences:** Negative past experiences, such as past betrayals or disappointments, can make individuals more guarded and inclined to prioritise themselves over others.

8. **Self-Gratification Culture:** In a world that often promotes instant gratification and self-indulgence, individuals can easily fall into selfish behaviour patterns as they pursue personal pleasure and comfort.
9. **Growth and Maturity:** Immaturity or lack of personal growth can contribute to selfish tendencies. As individuals develop emotionally and mentally, they are more likely to recognise the importance of considering others' needs.
10. **Entitlement:** A sense of entitlement can lead individuals to believe that their needs and desires should always take precedence. This can stem from a belief that they deserve special treatment.

Recognising the root causes of selfishness can be crucial in addressing it within a marriage. Couples can engage in open conversations, seek counselling, and work together to foster empathy and a deeper understanding of each other's perspectives. Overcoming selfish behaviour requires a commitment to personal growth, effective communication, and a shared dedication to building a strong and selfless partnership.

Open communication, empathy, and willingness to compromise are essential to address the impact of selfishness in a marriage. Couples can seek professional counselling or engage in constructive conversations to identify the root causes of selfish behaviour and work together to restore a healthy and thriving partnership.

The Essence of Christ's Unselfishness: *"For even the Son of Man did not come to be served, but to serve, and to give His life a ransom for many"* (Mark 10:45).

Christ's unselfishness is the cornerstone of our faith. His mission was not to seek His interests but to humbly serve humanity. His life exemplified selflessness—He healed the sick, comforted the broken-hearted, and laid down His life for our redemption. Embracing unselfishness means embodying the essence of Christ's love, compassion, and willingness to put others' needs before our own.

The Example of Christ's Humility: *"...but made Himself of no reputation, taking the form of a bondservant, and coming in the likeness of men"* (Philippians 2:7).

Saint Paul's words echo the profound humility of Christ. In His incarnation, Christ willingly set aside His divine glory, choosing to walk the path of a servant. His self-emptying nature challenges us to forsake selfish ambition and embrace the essence of unselfish love.

Christian Stories of Unselfish Love: The Gospels resound with stories of Christ's unselfish interactions. In the parable of the Good Samaritan, He highlighted the significance of caring for others, even those considered strangers. His ultimate unselfish act was His crucifixion—a sacrifice to redeem humanity from sin and death.

The Widow's Mite: In the bustling courtyard of the temple, Jesus observed a poor widow offering two small copper coins as her contribution *(Mark 12:41-44)*. While others gave out of abundance, her unselfish gift drew His attention. Jesus praised her, revealing that she had given more than all the rest, for her offering came from her heart.

Pope Shenouda III's teachings harmonise with Christ's unselfishness. His words echo the essence of Christ's teachings, inspiring us to conquer selfishness by embodying unselfishness in our daily lives. He encourages us to follow Christ's example of humility and selflessness, vital for fostering strong Christian families.

The Family as a Crucible of Unselfishness: Within the family, Christ's unselfishness finds expression through mutual love and sacrifice. Husbands and wives emulate Christ's relationship with His Church, marked by sacrificial love *(Ephesians 5:25)*. Parents model unselfishness as they care for their children, reflecting Christ's nurturing love for His flock.

Guided by Christ's unselfish love, grounded in the Scripture, and inspired by Pope Shenouda III's teachings, young Christian families are summoned to embody unselfishness. By reflecting on Christ's humility, valuing others' interests, and following His selfless example, we weave a tapestry of unselfish love resonating with the heart of our faith. May Christ's unselfishness, Scripture, and the guidance of Pope Shenouda III inspire us to live lives of service, humility, and love—a reflection of the unselfish love Christ bestowed upon us all.

When a Christian husband and wife embody unselfishness within their marriage, profound and transformative effects occur that align closely with the teachings of Christ. Here's how a Christian marriage flourishes when both partners prioritise unselfishness:

1. **Christ-Centred Unity:** Unselfishness in a Christian marriage strengthens the spiritual bond between spouses. Both partners recognise that their marriage reflects Christ's sacrificial love for His Church. They work together to create a unity rooted in Christ's teachings and characterised by mutual respect and selflessness.

2. **Living Gospel Values:** An unselfish marriage embodies Gospel values in action. Husbands and wives follow Christ's example of humility, love, and service. Their marriage becomes a living testimony to the power of Christ's teachings in transforming hearts and relationships.

3. **Mutual Submission:** Christian spouses practice mutual submission, as taught in Ephesians 5:21. They willingly defer to each other's needs and preferences, recognising that their marriage is a partnership where both are called to serve and support one another.

4. **Spiritual Growth:** Unselfishness fosters spiritual growth in both partners. They encourage each other to deepen their faith, pray and reflect, and seek God's guidance in their individual and joint endeavours.
5. **Forgiveness and Grace:** In an unselfish marriage, forgiveness, and grace flow freely. Spouses are quick to extend forgiveness, just as Christ forgives us. This creates an environment of healing and growth, preventing bitterness from taking root.
6. **Servant Leadership:** Husbands, inspired by Christ's servant leadership, lead their families with humility and love. They prioritise the well-being of their wives and children, setting an example of selflessness.
7. **Nurtured Love:** Unselfishness nurtures love that deepens over time. Both partners continually seek ways to express their love through acts of service, kind words, and thoughtful gestures, creating a strong foundation of affection and devotion.
8. **Shared Mission:** Christian spouses share a mission beyond their relationship—glorifying God through marriage. Their unselfish partnership becomes a testament to God's love and grace, inspiring others to pursue Christ-centred marriages.
9. **Generosity:** Unselfishness encourages a spirit of generosity in a Christian marriage. Both partners willingly share their time, resources, and talents with each other and those in need, following Christ's command to love our neighbours.
10. **Eternal Perspective:** Unselfishness reminds Christian couples of their eternal purpose. They focus on building a marriage that flourishes in this life and prepares them for an eternity with God.

In an unselfish Christian marriage, Christ's presence is palpable. His love permeates every aspect of the relationship, guiding husbands and wives to prioritise each other's well-being, just as Christ selflessly gave Himself for His Church. Through their unselfish love, Christian couples exemplify the transformative power of Christ's teachings and become beacons of hope and inspiration to others seeking to honour God through their unions.

The challenge of being unselfish is a fundamental yet complex issue that young Christian couples often face in their families. Balancing personal needs, ambitions, and desires with Christ's selflessness is a constant journey of growth, humility, and sacrifice.

Understanding the Challenge:

The call to be unselfish can clash with personal aspirations and societal pressures in a world that often promotes self-centeredness and individualism. Young Christian couples must navigate this challenge as they strive to create harmonious, loving, and Christ-centred family dynamics.

Impact on Relationships:

The challenge of being unselfish has a profound impact on young Christian couples and their families:

- **Marital Harmony:** Selfishness can lead to conflict, resentment, and misunderstanding within the marital relationship. Prioritising personal desires over the spouse's well-being can strain the bond between partners.

- **Parenting Approach:** Balancing personal interests with the needs of children can be challenging. Unselfish parenting requires sacrificing personal time and preferences to provide children with a nurturing and supportive environment.
- **Extended Family Dynamics:** The challenge extends to interactions with extended family members. Couples must balance commitments, expectations, and traditions while remaining united in their values.

Addressing the Challenge:

The model of Christ-like unselfishness should always be promoted in young families in many ways:

- **Model Christ's Example:** Emphasise Christ's selflessness as a role model. Encourage couples to study His teachings and actions to understand how they can imitate His sacrificial love in their own lives.
- **Communication:** Foster open communication between spouses. Encourage them to express their needs and concerns while actively listening to each other. Finding common ground can lead to solutions that honour both individuals' well-being.
- **Shared Goals:** Help each other identify shared goals and aspirations that align with their values. Working towards common objectives can strengthen their bond and foster a spirit of unity.
- **Prioritise Service:** Encourage acts of service within the family and community. Serving others together can create opportunities for shared experiences that promote selflessness.

- **Set Healthy Boundaries:** Discuss the importance of setting healthy boundaries to ensure each individual has time for personal growth and self-care while prioritising family needs.
- **Practice Gratitude:** Teach each other to practice gratitude for each other and the blessings they have. This can shift their focus away from personal desires and towards appreciation for the present.
- **Seek Wisdom:** Encourage each other to seek guidance from the church fathers, older couples, or trusted individuals who have navigated similar challenges. Learning from their experiences can provide valuable insights.

The challenge of being unselfish is a continuous journey of growth and self-discovery for young Christian couples. By embracing the example of Christ, fostering open communication, and prioritising service and unity, couples can create a harmonious and loving family environment that reflects the selfless love God desires for families. In their pursuit of unselfishness, couples strengthen their relationships and bear witness to the transformative power of Christ's love in their lives.

As we conclude our reflection on the profound virtue of unselfishness within the context of young Christian families, we transition to a cornerstone principle that underpins our entire journey—balancing our focus on the Kingdom of God. Just as unselfishness brings harmony within family dynamics, pursuing the Kingdom brings alignment to every facet of our lives.

In Chapter 23: "Balancing Focus on the Kingdom of God in Young Families," we embark on a journey that mirrors the delicate dance of life itself. Navigating the modern world's distractions and demands, young Christian families are called to seek the Kingdom of God first, trusting that all other aspects shall find their rightful place.

Guided by the teachings of Christ, the wisdom of scripture, and the testimony of families who have embraced this principle, this chapter unfolds as a roadmap to harmonise the temporal and the eternal. It offers insights into fostering spiritual growth, nurturing a deep relationship with God, and integrating faith into daily rhythms.

As we step into the realm of balancing our focus on the Kingdom of God, we invite you to join us on a path illuminated by Christ's eternal truths. Chapter 23 awaits—a chapter that beckons us to recalibrate our priorities, seek divine alignment, and anchor our families in the enduring embrace of the Kingdom.

Chapter 23

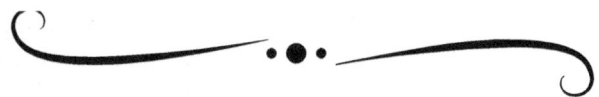

Balancing Focus on the Kingdom of God in Young Families

Every President Will Be a Footnote!

"Therefore, as we embrace the unshakable kingdom bestowed upon us, let us express gratitude for the grace that enables us to serve God acceptably, with deep reverence and godly fear" - Hebrews 12:28.

Above the world's nations, including America, stands the kingdom of our Lord Jesus. While earthly realms may tremble and their foundations shift, the sovereignty of Christ's kingdom remains unwavering. The very shaking these temporal domains experience serves a purpose: to reveal and uphold the eternal and unshakable truths.

Amid these quakes, we gaze upon the only steadfast kingdom and approach our worship with profound reverence and awe. Our sovereign and reigning King, Jesus Christ, is the pinnacle of stability and the foundation upon which we stand. In the eloquent words of John Piper, "One day, America and all its presidents will be a mere footnote in history, but God's kingdom will endure for eternity." What a statement?!

Contemplate this truth for a moment — it is both powerful and awe-inspiring. The sentiment above resonates deeply with me, and I wanted to share it with you, dear reader. It originates from John Piper, a luminary among righteous and impactful Christian authors of our modern era. He has graciously nurtured a remarkable ministry called "Desiring God," an endeavour that has enriched countless lives.

In the middle of complicated threads of daily life, where responsibilities, dreams, and aspirations intertwine, young Christian families encounter the profound challenge of nurturing an unwavering focus on the Kingdom of God. In a world brimming with distractions and demands, this endeavour is akin to navigating a delicate dance that necessitates constant discernment, aligning our earthly pursuits with the eternal.

The Gospel, according to Saint Matthew, unveils a timeless principle that resonates deeply with the hearts of young families seeking equilibrium amidst life's multifaceted demands: *"But seek first the kingdom of God and His righteousness, and all these things shall be added to you"* (Matthew 6:33). These words, spoken by Christ Himself, are not mere advice; they are a divine compass guiding us toward the essence of balance.

Embracing this principle, we find that the Kingdom of God is not merely a distant realm to be attained in the afterlife; it is a reality woven into our existence's very fabric. It is the light that illuminates our decisions, the foundation that shapes our relationships, and the purpose that infuses every aspect of our lives with meaning.

Allow me to share a story that illustrates the transformative power of seeking the Kingdom in the midst of life's demands:

Balancing Focus on the Kingdom of God in Young Families

In a bustling city lived a young couple, David and Emily. Both deeply committed to their careers and dedicated to raising their children, they found their days brimming with responsibilities. Yet, as their lives swirled with activity, they recognised the need for a renewed focus on the eternal.

One evening, while reading Matthew 6:33 together, a thought ignited within them—a desire to live out these words in practical ways. David suggested they allocate a portion of their weekly schedule for family prayer, reading scripture, and engaging in acts of kindness within their community. Emily wholeheartedly agreed, and together, they embarked on a journey to seek the Kingdom as a family.

As weeks turned into months, David and Emily discovered that their shared focus on the Kingdom brought about a remarkable shift. The moments of family prayer became anchors of unity and spiritual nourishment. Reading scripture together deepened their understanding of God's purposes. Engaging in community service as a family transformed their perspective on their role within their city.

They realised that seeking the Kingdom wasn't a separate task but a lens through which they approached every aspect of life. Their children witnessed firsthand the beauty of a family centred on Christ's teachings, and they, too, began to embrace the joy of seeking the Kingdom.

The teachings of early church fathers resonate with this approach. St. John Chrysostom aptly noted, *"The kingdom of God is not meat and drink, but righteousness, and peace, and joy in the Holy Ghost"* (Romans 14:17). Here, we discover that the Kingdom enriches not just our personal lives, but our interactions with others and the atmosphere we create around us.

Saint Anthony the Great, renowned for his wisdom and ascetic life, echoes the call to prioritise the eternal. He once said, *"Our life and death are with our neighbour. If we gain our brother, we have gained God, but if we scandalise our brother, we have sinned against Christ."* This wisdom underscores that seeking the Kingdom is inseparable from our relationships and interactions in the world.

The question arises: Why is it so important to adopt this mindset? The answer is found in the very nature of our existence. When we place the Kingdom of God at the forefront of our hearts, minds and actions, our lives have a transcendent purpose. Our priorities realign, our decisions gain clarity, and our relationships flourish with love and compassion. By seeking the Kingdom first, we infuse our daily routines with divine significance, turning the mundane into the sacred.

Balancing the demands of daily life with an unwavering focus on the Kingdom is a continuous endeavour. We may falter, but the grace of God lifts us. We may waver, but the truth of Matthew 6:33 steadies our course. Pursuing the Kingdom enriches our lives, filling them with purpose, joy, and a deep sense of alignment with God's divine plan.

As you embark on this journey, let the guiding principle be clear: Seek the Kingdom of God first. Let your faith illuminate your steps, shaping your decisions, relationships, and aspirations. May the Kingdom's light shine through you, infusing your family's path with the radiant glow of divine purpose, and may you find unshakeable balance in the embrace of His eternal presence.

The challenge of being focused on the Kingdom of God is a significant endeavour that young Christian families encounter in their pursuit of living out their faith. The tension between earthly responsibilities and eternal priorities requires intentional effort, wisdom, a deep understanding of God's kingdom principles, and, above all, a balance of priorities and focus.

Understanding the Challenge:

Young families often struggle to balance their earthly commitments—such as career, education, and family life—with the call to seek the Kingdom of God first. The world's demands and distractions can easily divert attention from eternal values.

Impact on Faith and Relationships:

The challenge of focusing on the Kingdom of God can influence young families in various ways:
- **Spiritual Priorities:** Juggling the demands of daily life can lead to unintentional neglect of spiritual disciplines and growth, potentially weakening their connection to God.
- **Materialism:** Pursuing material success and financial security can overshadow the importance of investing in spiritual and Kingdom-oriented pursuits.
- **Time Allocation:** Balancing work, family, and other commitments can leave little time for actively participating in church, community, and Kingdom-building activities.

Addressing the Challenge:

- **Align with God's Priorities:** Encourage and lead your family to regularly assess their priorities and consider whether their pursuits align with God's Kingdom values. This can help them make intentional decisions.

- **Cultivate a Kingdom Perspective:** Teach your family to view their daily responsibilities as opportunities to serve God's Kingdom. A Kingdom perspective transforms mundane tasks into meaningful contributions.
- **Prioritise Spiritual Disciplines:** Stress the importance of regular prayer, Scripture study, worship, and quality fellowship time. These practices anchor families in their faith and deepen their relationship with God.
- **Family Worship:** Promote family worship "family altar" and devotion times. Gathering as a family to pray, read the Bible, and discuss spiritual matters nurtures a Kingdom-centred atmosphere at home.
- **Generosity:** Encourage everyone in your family to adopt a spirit of generosity by sharing their resources with others in need. This aligns with God's heart for the marginalised and helps families contribute to the Kingdom's growth.
- **Invest in Relationships:** Emphasise the significance of building relationships within the church community. These connections provide spiritual support, encouragement, and accountability.
- **Time Management:** Help your family, especially your children, learn how to manage their time effectively by setting boundaries and allocating time for earthly responsibilities and Kingdom-building pursuits.
- **Seek God's Guidance:** Encourage your family to seek God's guidance in decision-making and, through their confession father's guidance. Praying for wisdom and discernment ensures that their choices align with God's plan by continuously seeking God's will in all their matters and life decisions.

Balancing Focus on the Kingdom of God in Young Families

The challenge of being focused on the Kingdom of God is a transformative journey that requires intentionality, a heart of surrender, and an unwavering commitment to God's eternal principles. By aligning their pursuits with Kingdom values, investing in spiritual growth, and seeking to contribute to God's work, young Christian families can navigate the complexities of life while keeping their eyes fixed on the ultimate goal of advancing God's Kingdom on earth. In doing so, they become agents of change, bearing witness to the profound impact of living with an eternal perspective.

As we conclude our exploration of balancing the focus on the Kingdom of God within young families, we transition to a pivotal aspect of nurturing a solid spiritual foundation: intentionally allocating time to God. Just as a ship requires a well-charted course to reach its destination, young Christian families must allocate time in their lives to foster a deeper connection with their Creator. Join us in Chapter 24 as we delve into the profound significance of dedicating time to God's presence and how this practice strengthens not only individual faith but also the bonds within the family unit.

Chapter 24

Allocating Time to God in the Lives of Young Christian Families

In the bustling tapestry of modern life, where time often seems to slip through our fingers like sand, young Christian families face the challenge of allocating meaningful moments to commune with God. Amidst the whirlwind of responsibilities, work, and countless commitments, carving out time for God can feel daunting. Yet, as we delve into the treasure trove of the Bible and the stories of faithful figures, we discover the profound significance of reserving a space for God in our lives.

The Scripture beckons us to consider the importance of time devoted to the divine: "But those who wait on the Lord shall renew their strength; they shall mount up with wings like eagles, they shall run and not be weary, they shall walk and not faint." (Isaiah 40:31, NKJV) In this verse, we find an invitation to seek God's presence, a promise of renewal, and the assurance that time invested in Him yields abundant blessings.

Reflect upon the story of Mary and Martha, two sisters who welcomed Jesus into their home. As Martha busied herself with the preparations, Mary chose to sit at the Lord's feet, listening to His teachings. While Martha's actions were not amiss, Jesus gently reminded her that Mary had chosen *"the good part"* (Luke 10:42). This narrative encapsulates the essence of allocating time to God—to be still, listen, and commune with Him.

As the psalmist proclaims, *"Be still, and know that I am God; I will be exalted among the nations, I will be exalted in the earth!"* (Psalm 46:10). Amid the tumult of life, taking moments of stillness to recognise God's presence not only nurtures our souls but also amplifies our ability to navigate the challenges that come our way.

Let us draw inspiration from the story of Daniel, a man of unyielding faith who consistently set aside time for prayer even in the face of persecution. His commitment to maintaining a sacred rhythm of connecting with God underscored the importance of prioritising divine communion—even when circumstances were adverse.

As young Christian families, the deliberate allocation of time to God bears manifold benefits. It enhances our spiritual vitality, fostering a deeper relationship with the Creator. It instils purpose and perspective, grounding our actions in eternal truth. Moreover, it becomes a legacy for the next generation, teaching them the immeasurable value of making room for God amidst life's busyness.

A poignant saying attributed to the desert father St. Moses the Black captures the essence of this practice: *"Sit in your cell, and your cell will teach you everything."* In the quietness of contemplation, God imparts wisdom, guidance, and a sense of His abiding presence.

Allocating Time to God in the Lives of Young Christian Families

Consider the image of a family sitting around the dinner table, each member sharing the joys and challenges of their day. Now, envision this sacred space expanding to encompass prayer, scripture reading, and reflection moments. Just as nourishment sustains our bodies, spiritual nourishment nourishes our souls, fostering a deep connection with God and one another.

In a world that clamours for our attention, the deliberate act of allocating time to God serves as a powerful counterbalance. It reminds us that amidst the cacophony of life, there is a sanctified space where we can draw close to the Divine, finding solace, guidance, and the assurance that God's presence enriches every facet of our existence.

Saint Macarius the Great wisely stated, *"The soul who loves God always has its mind lifted to Him, and is not afraid of anything, and does not fear anything, because he is united to the One who is immortal and eternal."* This beautiful insight underscores the transformative power of allocating time to God—to be united with the unchanging One amid life's transient currents.

Pope Shenouda III, the beloved leader of the Coptic Orthodox Church, emphasised the significance of allocating time to God in his wise saying: *"Time with God is the essence of life."* This profound statement encapsulates the truth that our moments spent in communion with God hold immeasurable value, shaping our lives and guiding our paths.

As you navigate the complexities of life, may you carve out moments to be still before God. As the psalmist urges, *"Oh, taste and see that the Lord is good; blessed is the man who trusts in Him!"* (Psalm 34:8) may you find blessing in the sweet communion with your Creator. By allocating time to God, may you discover His wisdom's riches, His love's fullness, and the grace to navigate life's journey with unwavering faith.

The challenge of allocating time to God is a significant concern for young Christian families in today's fast-paced world. Amidst busy schedules, commitments, and distractions, finding time for spiritual practices and nurturing a deep relationship with God can be a formidable challenge.

Understanding the Challenge:

Young families often find themselves pulled in multiple directions by work, parenting responsibilities, social obligations, and leisure activities. Amidst these demands, setting aside meaningful time for God can become a struggle, leading to spiritual stagnation and a sense of disconnect.

Impact on Faith and Relationships:

The challenge of allocating time to God can have several consequences on young Christian families:

- **Spiritual Dryness**: Neglecting consistent time with God can lead to a lack of spiritual nourishment, resulting in spiritual dryness and weakening faith.
- **Shallow Relationships:** An absence of intentional time with God can affect the depth of a family's relationship with Him, hindering their ability to experience His presence and guidance.
- **Inconsistent Values:** Without regular exposure to God's Word and principles, families may unknowingly drift away from the values that anchor their faith.

Addressing the Challenge:

Guide your family in addressing the challenge of allocating time to God within their busy lives:

- **Prioritise God:** Encourage everyone in your family to view time with God as a priority rather than an afterthought. Setting aside intentional time demonstrates their commitment to nurturing their relationship with Him. Start while children are young, practice it diligently, and be convinced yourself while practising it.
- **Establish Routine:** Recommend establishing a daily routine that includes dedicated time for prayer, Scripture reading, and reflection. Consistency helps develop a habit of seeking God daily.
- **Family Altar:** Suggest incorporating the family alter times into the daily schedule. This could involve reading a Bible passage together, discussing its meaning, and praying as a family.
- **Digital Detox:** Encourage your family to periodically disconnect from technology and social media to create space for quiet reflection and focused time with God.
- **Start Small:** Acknowledge that carving out significant chunks of time may be challenging initially. Starting with shorter periods and gradually increasing them can make the transition smoother.
- **Accountability**: Encourage family members to hold each other accountable for their commitment to spending time with God. Sharing their progress and struggles can provide mutual support.
- **Utilise Free Moments:** Encourage family members to use small pockets of free time for prayer and reflection throughout the day. These moments can add up and

contribute to spiritual growth. We call it " Gather up the fragments" John 6:12

- **Integrate Faith:** Suggest integrating faith into daily activities. Praying while commuting, listening to worship music, or reflecting on Scripture during breaks can help families stay connected to God.

The challenge of allocating time to God is critical to nurturing a vibrant Christian faith within young families. By intentionally prioritising God, establishing routines, and leveraging available moments, families can overcome the constraints of their busy lives and create a space for spiritual growth. As they invest time developing their relationship with God, they can experience His transformative presence, deepen their faith, and draw closer to His heart.

Having explored the crucial practice of allocating time to God within the lives of young Christian families, we now turn our attention to a topic that resonates deeply with the ever-evolving dynamics of faith and culture: Navigating Identity Challenges in Christian Families. In a world that often challenges our values and beliefs, young families are tasked with preserving their Christian identity while embracing the diversity and complexities of the modern age. Join us in Chapter 25 as we journey to uncover the wisdom, principles, and timeless truths that guide families in navigating this delicate balance between unwavering faith and the winds of change.

Chapter 25

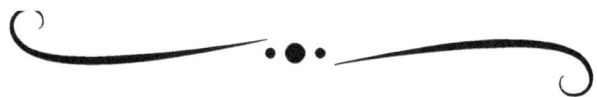

Navigating Identity Challenges in Christian Families

In a world that often defines identity through ever-shifting cultural trends and external influences, young Christian families encounter a unique challenge: maintaining a firm, Christ-centred identity amidst the tides of change. The journey of self-discovery and identity formation can be complex, predominantly when guided by values that may contrast prevailing norms. As we navigate this intricate path, we find solace and guidance in the timeless wisdom of the Bible, which speaks directly to the essence of our identity as children of God.

Defining Christian Identity

At the heart of Christian identity lies the fundamental recognition that we are, first and foremost, children of God. It is a profound understanding that transcends fleeting societal labels and temporal categorisations. Christian identity is rooted in the belief that each individual is fearfully and wonderfully made, bearing the imprint of the Creator's craftsmanship.

The Apostle Paul's words ring with clarity and assurance: *"For you are all sons of God through faith in Christ Jesus"* (Galatians 3:26). This declaration transcends the ephemeral constructs of this world, reminding us that our true identity is rooted in our relationship with Christ. This foundational truth becomes the cornerstone upon which we build our understanding of self, family, and purpose.

Navigating Challenges

The journey of nurturing a Christian identity involves navigating challenges that seek to reshape and redefine who we are. It entails acknowledging the cultural currents that may attempt to divert us from our divine calling. Yet, with our Christian identity as an anchor, we are equipped to stand firm against these tides and live purposefully.

Consider the narrative of Daniel, a young man who found himself amidst a foreign culture that sought to redefine his identity. Despite the pressures to conform, he remained steadfast in his faith and commitment to God's commandments. His identity as a servant of God superseded any external labels, leading him to a life of integrity and influence.

A Precious Identity

In a culture that often prioritises self-expression and individualism, the Apostle Peter's words guide us: *"But you are a chosen generation, a royal priesthood, a holy nation, His own special people, that you may proclaim the praises of Him who called you out of darkness into His marvellous light"* (1 Peter 2:9). This divine calling sets us apart and infuses our identity with purpose—to proclaim God's praises and reflect His light.

The Significance for Our Children:

Amid a world that bombards our children with messages of self-worth tied to appearances, achievements, and external validation, the importance of nurturing a Christian identity becomes even more pronounced. Our children are growing up in an era where digital media, societal pressures, and ever-changing trends relentlessly mould their identities.

We instil a strong Christian identity in our children and give them an unshakable foundation. This identity transcends the superficial and rests securely in their identity as God's beloved creations. This identity is not based on fleeting measures of success, popularity, or appearances. Instead, it is rooted in the unchanging truth of their worth as individuals cherished by God.

A Beacon of Light:

As young Christian families, embracing our identity in Christ requires intentional effort. It involves instilling in our children a deep understanding of their worth as beloved creations of God. It involves fostering a sense of belonging to the larger family of faith—a family that spans across generations and cultures.

In a world where identity can be fleeting, let us draw inspiration from the unchanging truth of Scripture. Let us recognise that our identity in Christ is a gift that empowers us to live lives of purpose, integrity, and influence. Just as the apostle Paul encourages, "For you died, and your life is hidden with Christ in God." (Colossians 3:3, NKJV), may our identity be rooted in Christ and our lives reflect His transforming love.

As you navigate the ever-evolving landscape of identity, may you and your family find strength, purpose, and security in your shared identity as children of the King. During challenges and shifting cultural norms, may your Christ-centred identity be a beacon of light, guiding you to live authentically, love deeply, and walk confidently in the path God ordained for you.

Empowering children to acquire a Christian identity involves intentional nurturing, guidance, and modelling of faith-based values. Empowering children to acquire a Christian identity is a gradual process that requires consistent effort and patience. By actively incorporating these practices like Scripture and Prayer, church Involvement, modelling Christ-like behaviour, teaching and reinforcing Christian values, services and compassions, open communications, sharing faith stories, the life of saints stories, family and Coptic traditions, cultivating gratitude and age-appropriate discipleship into your family's life, you can create an environment where your children grow in their understanding of their faith and their identity as beloved children of God.

The challenge of identity is a profound issue that impacts young Christian families in a world marked by shifting cultural norms, individualism, and conflicting value systems. Defining and maintaining a Christ-centred identity amid societal pressures requires intentional reflection, grounded faith, and a commitment to biblical principles.

Understanding the Challenge:

Young Christian families grapple with the challenge of establishing and nurturing an identity rooted in Christ while being influenced by diverse cultural, social, and ideological perspectives. The tension between upholding Christian values and conforming to secular norms can lead to identity confusion.

Impact on Faith and Relationships:

The challenge of identity can affect young Christian families in various ways:

- **Spiritual Clarity:** Without a firm understanding of their identity in Christ, families may struggle to align their actions, decisions, and relationships with biblical values.
- **Marital Unity:** Differing perceptions of identity can lead to conflicts and misunderstandings within marriage, especially when spouses have varying perspectives on their roles and responsibilities.
- **Parental Influence:** Parents' own identity struggles can inadvertently impact their children's perception of themselves and their faith, potentially hindering the transmission of a solid Christian identity.

Addressing the Challenge:

Guide young Christian family members in addressing the challenge of identity by fostering a Christ-cantered identity within their family unit:

- **Rooted in Scripture:** Encourage your family to ground their identity in the truth of Scripture. Regular Bible study helps them understand their identity as beloved children of God.
- **Family Mission Statement:** Suggest creating a family mission statement that outlines core values and principles based on biblical teachings. This provides a clear identity framework.
- **Open Dialogue:** Foster open discussions within the family about identity and values. Encourage family members to share their thoughts, feelings, and questions about their identity journey.
- **Reflection and Prayer:** Recommend intentional reflection and prayer, allowing family members to seek God's guidance in understanding their unique identities and purposes.
- **Church Community:** Emphasise the importance of being part of a supportive church community and services. This provides a sense of belonging and reinforces a shared identity in Christ.
- **Cultural Discernment:** Teach families to discern cultural messages and trends through the lens of their Christian identity. This helps them make choices that align with their faith.
- **Positive Role Models:** Highlight the significance of identifying and learning from positive role models within the church who exemplify a Christ-centred identity.

- **Parental Modelling:** Parents are always encouraged to model a Christ-centred identity by consistently living out their faith demonstrating love, humility, and servant leadership within the family.

The identity challenge is a deeply personal and transformative journey for young Christian families. Families can navigate the complexities of identity formation by anchoring their identity in Christ, reflecting on their values, and engaging in intentional conversations. A Christ-centred identity strengthens family bonds and equips families to live out their faith boldly, make decisions that align with their values, and positively impact their communities and the world.

As we conclude our exploration of Navigating Identity Challenges in Christian Families, we transition to a vital aspect of harmonious living: Embracing Contentment and Establishing Priorities for a Balanced Life. In a world that often breeds discontentment and urges us to pursue more relentlessly, the pursuit of balance and contentment becomes a transformative endeavour. Join us in Chapter 26 as we delve into the art of finding contentment amidst life's challenges and discover how aligning our priorities with God's design can lead to a life of purpose, fulfilment, and lasting joy.

Chapter 26

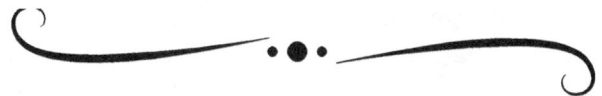

Embracing Contentment and Establishing Priorities for a Balanced Life

In a touching encounter, I was blessed to receive a profound lesson in contentment from a remarkable young lady. As I arrived to pick up my grandson Joshua from school, I had the privilege of meeting this lady—a captivating blend of Italian and Brazilian heritage. She introduced herself as a mother to a delightful daughter who shared the same kindergarten class as my grandson.

As our conversation deepened, I learned of a challenging reality. The young lady's little child bore the weight of a degenerative eye condition, one that was poised to rob her of sight in one eye. In the face of such adversity, her perspective was both humbling and enlightening.

With a spirit fortified by faith, she shared her daily practice. Each morning, she drew strength from the Lord, asking

Him to, according to her words, "put me on the right track," intentionally redirecting her focus towards the blessings she possessed rather than dwelling on the things she lacked. Her eyes glistened with a blend of determination and gratitude as she spoke of this simple yet profound ritual.

In her own words, she acknowledged the prevailing tendency to fall into the trap of fixating on what one lacks. She astutely recognised the struggle inherent in this pattern of thinking. Her wisdom revealed the elegant beauty of her approach—a practice anchored in gratitude and trust.

Her story resonates deeply as a poignant reminder of the power of contentment; yes contentment has a profound power. Her example illuminated the pathway to genuine joy—a path that doesn't hinge on accumulating possessions or fleeting desires. Instead, her practice showcases the profound truth that contentment is found in embracing the present moment, acknowledging the gifts we've been given, and nurturing a godly heart of gratitude.

Indeed, that's a profound and touching story that beautifully illustrates the essence of contentment. The young lady's perspective serves as a potent reminder that true contentment doesn't come from material possessions or the pursuit of what we lack but from appreciating and being grateful for the blessings we have been given. Her practice of drawing strength from the Lord each morning and focusing on what she has rather than what she doesn't have reflects deep spiritual wisdom.

Her story resonates with the teachings of Scripture and the wisdom of the early Church Fathers. It's a testament to the transformative power of gratitude and the ability to find contentment during challenges. By focusing on the goodness of God and the blessings in her life, she demonstrates resilience and an unwavering faith that guides her through difficulties. Amidst the complexities of life, she exudes a remarkable simplicity that is anything but ordinary. Her journey is a testimony to the transformative potential of faith and gratitude, a living embodiment of the words, *"I have learned to be content in whatever circumstances I am"* (Philippians 4:11).

This young lady's example shines as a beacon of light in a world often driven by the pursuit of more. Her attitude encourages us all to cultivate a heart of contentment, rooted in faith and gratitude, so we can find joy and peace regardless of our circumstances. Her practice of focusing on what she has rather than what she lacks serves as an inspiring reminder that true contentment comes from within, and it's a gift that we can cultivate through our relationship with God.

In the bustling tapestry of modern existence, where responsibilities pull us in countless directions, pursuing a balanced life is an enduring aspiration. Within this pursuit, two guiding stars emerge—contentment and priorities. These powerful concepts, rooted in ageless wisdom and anchored in faith, illuminate the path to a life of harmony, purpose, and fulfilment. As young families navigate the complexities of their roles and relationships, embracing contentment and establishing God-centred priorities become cornerstones of their journey toward equilibrium.

The Beauty of Contentment

At the heart of a balanced life lies the jewel of contentment. It is the art of finding joy and gratitude in the present moment, recognising the abundance surrounding us, and resting in the assurance that God's providence is ever-present. As the apostle Paul shares in Philippians 4:11-12, *"I have learned in whatever state I am, to be content: I know how to be abased, and I know how to abound. Everywhere and in all things I have learned both to be full and to be hungry, both to abound and to suffer need."* Through the lens of contentment, young families are invited to cherish the blessings of family, love, and faith, fostering an attitude that radiates peace and grace.

Contentment in Action: A Lesson from the Sparrow

In a quaint village nestled amidst rolling hills, lived a humble family. Samuel, a young father, worked tirelessly as a carpenter, and his wife, Abigail, cared for their children with unwavering love. Despite the challenges that life presented, an aura of contentment enveloped their home.

One summer evening, as the family gathered around the dinner table, their youngest daughter, Hannah, looked out the window. With eyes wide open, she exclaimed, "Look, a sparrow just built a nest on our windowsill!" The family approached the window with gentle curiosity. Indeed, a small sparrow had meticulously crafted a nest, woven with twigs and grass, just inches from the windowpane.

As the days turned into weeks, the family watched with fascination as the mother sparrow tended to her eggs, sheltering them from wind and rain. One morning, Hannah rushed into the house, her face beaming. *"The eggs hatched, Mom and Dad! There are tiny chicks in the nest!"* Samuel, Abigail, and their children shared the joy of this simple marvel of nature.

As the weeks passed, the family observed the sparrow parents tirelessly feeding their chicks, nurturing them into independence. Samuel turned to Abigail and said, *"Look at those sparrows, my love. They have so little, yet they embrace their role with dedication and contentment. We are blessed with a roof over our heads, food on our table, and the love that binds us together. Let us learn from the sparrows and treasure the blessings we have."*

From that day forward, the family carried the sparrow story in their hearts. It became a reminder that contentment is not found in accumulating possessions, but in embracing the beauty of each moment, cherishing the love that surrounds us, and trusting in God's provision.

Together, let us delve into the profound wisdom that contentment and priorities bring. May their lessons illuminate the way, infusing our lives with tranquillity, purpose, and a deepened connection to our faith. As we explore these chapters, may we discover that a balanced life is not a distant dream but a tangible reality—an invitation to journey toward wholeness, with contentment as our companion and God-cantered priorities as our guiding light

Cultivating Contentment: Embracing God's Abundant Blessings

Amid a world that often measures success by material possessions, cultivating contentment is a profound virtue for young Christian families. The pursuit of contentment invites us to shift our focus from the fleeting desires of consumerism to the enduring riches of God's love, grace, and provision. This chapter delves into the beauty of contentment, offering insights, Bible verses, and stories that guide young families toward embracing a life marked by gratitude and spiritual fulfilment.

Finding Joy in God's Provision

Drawing inspiration from the biblical story of the Israelites in the wilderness, we learn a valuable lesson about finding joy in God's provision. As God provided manna daily, the Israelites relied on His sustenance. This story echoes a timeless truth: contentment arises when we trust God's faithful provision, even when our circumstances appear uncertain.

Gratitude in Abundance and Scarcity

In the parable of the prodigal son, we witness the journey from abundance to scarcity and the transformational power of gratitude. When the prodigal son returns to his father, he learns that contentment flows not from indulgence but from embracing the love and acceptance that await him. This narrative reminds us that gratitude is the key to finding contentment regardless of circumstances.

Contentment as a Family Value

Instilling contentment as a family value involves intentionally shifting our focus from material accumulation to spiritual growth. Engaging in acts of gratitude, practising generosity, and fostering a sense of sufficiency create an environment where contentment thrives. 1 Timothy 6:6 reinforces this truth: "Now godliness with contentment is great gain."

Prioritising Eternal Treasures

Our Lord Jesus' teachings continually emphasise earthly treasures' impermanence and heavenly treasures' eternal value. Matthew 6:19-21 underscores this message: *"Lay up for yourselves treasures in heaven, where neither moth nor rust destroys and where thieves do not break in and steal."* By prioritising eternal treasures, we foster contentment that transcends the temporal.

Nurturing Contentment in Children

Teaching children the value of contentment is vital to nurturing balanced Christian families. Embrace the parable of the rich young ruler as an opportunity to discuss the dangers of excessive attachment to possessions. Encourage your children to find joy in simple blessings and to cultivate a heart that values relationships and spiritual growth above all else.

Embracing Simplicity and Sharing

In Acts 4:32-35, we witness the early Christian community embracing a life marked by simplicity and shared resources. Their unity and willingness to meet each other's needs reflect the profound contentment that arises when material possessions take a back seat to spiritual connection and communal well-being.

Daily Practices for Contentment

Practical steps for cultivating contentment can be woven into daily life. Family prayers of gratitude, regular reflections on God's blessings, and intentionally seeking opportunities to give back help shape an attitude of contentment within your family.

Contentment and Joy in Christ

Ultimately, contentment finds its deepest source in a relationship with Christ. Recognising that He is our ultimate source of joy and fulfilment empowers us to live contentedly, embracing His love and grace in every circumstance.

In a world that promotes constant striving for more, cultivating contentment becomes a revolutionary act—a testament to our trust in God's provision and our belief that true abundance flows from spiritual richness. As young Christian families, may you journey toward contentment with hearts filled with gratitude, recognising the immeasurable blessings that God has bestowed upon you. May your homes be places of joy, simplicity, and spiritual growth, where contentment becomes a treasured family value that shapes the way you live and love.

Cultivating contentment is particularly crucial for young families in today's fast-paced and consumer-driven world. Here's why:

1. **The foundation of lasting joy:** Contentment offers a foundation for genuine joy that is not dependent on external circumstances. Teaching children from a young age that happiness is not derived solely from material possessions empowers them to find joy in the intangible blessings of life.

2. **Counteracting Materialism:** In a culture that glorifies materialism and constant consumption, instilling contentment helps young families resist the pressure to seek material acquisition more constantly. This counteracts the cycle of always wanting more and encourages a focus on what truly matters.

3. **Financial Well-being:** Cultivating contentment can contribute to financial well-being. Young families often face financial pressures as they establish their

households. Prioritising contentment helps them make mindful financial decisions, avoid unnecessary debt, and allocate resources wisely.

4. **Stronger Relationships:** A contented family is more likely to focus on building strong relationships with each other and with God. As they embrace a spirit of gratitude, they become more attentive to the needs of others, fostering deeper connections and empathy within the family.

5. **Faith Development:** Contentment aligns with the teachings of Jesus to prioritise heavenly treasures over earthly ones. Teaching young family members to find fulfilment in Christ rather than material possessions nurtures their spiritual growth and faith journey.

6. **Stress Reduction:** Contentment reduces stress and anxiety caused by pursuing an elusive "more." By embracing a simpler lifestyle and finding contentment in what they have, young families can experience greater peace of mind.

7. **Modelling Values:** Children learn by observing their parents' attitudes and behaviours. When parents model contentment, children are more likely to adopt this attitude themselves. This invaluable lesson equips them to navigate challenges and uncertainties with grace.

8. **Resilience:** Contentment builds resilience by teaching young families to adapt and find joy regardless of circumstances. This resilience serves as a vital tool in facing life's inevitable ups and downs.

9. **Stronger Sense of Identity:** Young families prioritising contentment often develop a stronger sense of identity based on their faith, values, and relationships rather than external markers of success.

10. **Generosity and Compassion:** A contented family is more likely to engage in acts of generosity and compassion as they understand the value of sharing their blessings with others. This reinforces Christian values of love, service, and caring for those in need.
11. **Joy in Simplicity:** Contentment encourages young families to find joy in the simplicity of life. This can lead to more meaningful experiences, quality time spent together, and a deeper appreciation for the beauty around them.

In a world that encourages constant comparison, competition, and acquisition, nurturing contentment in young families is an antidote to these pressures. It creates an environment where love, faith, and gratitude flourish, setting the stage for a fulfilling and purpose-driven family life.

Cultivating Contentment: The Coptic Way of Finding Joy in Simplicity

In the serene expanse of the Coptic Orthodox tradition, the concept of contentment radiates with a timeless wisdom that resonates deeply in the hearts of young Christian families. In our Coptic Orthodoxy tradition and culture contentment embodies a spirit of serene satisfaction and gratitude for God's blessings upon His children. Perhaps this's rooted in ancient teachings, nourished by our rich monastic teachings from the early church Fathers; stories upheld by earlier generations, the Coptic approach to contentment offers a transformative perspective on life's challenges and blessings alike.

Gratitude as the Heart of Contentment

At the heart of the Coptic understanding of contentment lies unwavering gratitude to God. No wonder we start every liturgical prayer in our sacramental diversity with the thanksgiving prayer. Just as the Psalms overflow with thanksgiving, the Coptic Orthodox tradition emphasises the importance of giving thanks for both abundance and scarcity. In this spirit, young families are encouraged to cultivate a heart of gratitude, finding solace in knowing that a loving and providential God orchestrates every circumstance.

Simplicity in Material and Spiritual Aspects

The ascetic tradition cherished within Coptic Orthodoxy serves as a poignant reminder of the value of simplicity. Drawing inspiration from the desert fathers and mothers, young families are guided toward a life unburdened by excessive possessions. This simplicity extends not only to material belongings but also to the spiritual realm, emphasising the purity of heart that comes from uncluttered devotion to God.

Trust in God's Providence

The Coptic way of contentment is firmly rooted in trust in God's providence. Just as God clothes the lilies of the field, the Coptic faithful are taught to rely on His loving care. Through the teachings of spiritual fathers like St. Anthony the Great, young families are encouraged to release anxiety and embrace the comforting truth that God provides for His children.

Embracing the Cross

The Coptic Orthodox tradition greatly emphasises embracing the cross as a path to spiritual growth. Just as the cross stands at the centre of Coptic churches, it also serves as a symbol of endurance and transformation in the lives of young families. Embracing challenges with faith and resilience, Coptic families discover that true contentment often emerges from the crucible of trials.

Prayer as a Source of Contentment

In the Coptic tradition, prayer is a source of profound contentment and communion with God. Our "Agpeya," a treasured prayer book, offers a structured rhythm of psalms and prayers that guide families to find solace and strength in conversation with the Divine. As young families engage in the rhythmic recitations of the Agpeya, they are reminded that contentment flourishes in the fertile soil of intimate communion with God.

Passing down the Legacy

The Coptic tradition of contentment is a legacy that spans generations. From the lives of the desert fathers to the modern Coptic faithful, the torch of contentment is passed down through stories, practices, and faith. Young families are encouraged to embrace this legacy, weaving the thread of contentment into the fabric of their daily lives and nurturing it as a precious inheritance for their children.

In the tapestry of Coptic Orthodoxy, contentment is a radiant thread that weaves together faith, gratitude, simplicity, and trust. Young Christian families who embrace the Coptic way of contentment find themselves walking a path that leads to a deeper connection with God, a profound appreciation for life's blessings, and a tranquillity that transcends the challenges of this world. Just as the saints of old discovered, true contentment is a treasure found in the embrace of Christ's love and the unending wellspring of His grace.

Establishing God-Centred Priorities in Young Families

Young families often juggle numerous roles and obligations in the intricate dance of life's demands and responsibilities. Amid these challenges, pursuing God-centred priorities becomes essential for maintaining harmony, fostering spiritual growth, and nurturing strong relationships. This chapter delves into the art of establishing priorities that align with God's design for families, offering guidance, practical insights, and biblical foundations.

The Foundation of Priorities

At the core of establishing priorities is recognising that God is the ultimate source of guidance. This divine wisdom serves as a steadfast anchor in the ever-changing sea of choices and decisions that young families encounter. Seeking His wisdom through prayer and delving into His Word equips families with the tools to navigate life's complexities with clarity and purpose. Proverbs 3:5-6 (NKJV) encapsulates this principle: "Trust in the Lord with all your heart, and lean not on your own understanding; in all your ways acknowledge Him, and He shall direct your paths."

Identifying Core Values

Clarifying core Christian values as a family is essential to setting priorities that resonate with God's heart. By identifying values that align with their Christian faith and beliefs, young families can make intentional choices that reflect their commitment to God's teachings. This process involves open communication, deep reflection, and a collective agreement on what matters most in light of His divine commandments.

Balancing Faith, Family, and Work

Finding equilibrium among faith, family, and work is a delicate dance that young families strive to master. Learning from the example of Jesus, who skilfully balanced His ministry with moments of solitude and prayer, families are encouraged to allocate time for nurturing their relationship with God. Mark 1:35 reminds us: *"Now in the morning, having risen a long while before daylight, He went out and departed to a solitary place, and there He prayed."*

Nurturing Marital and Parental Bonds

Prioritising the well-being of marital and parental relationships is fundamental to fostering a God-centred home. A strong and loving marriage provides a nurturing foundation for children to witness and learn about love, respect, and teamwork. Ephesians 5:25 guides husbands: *"Husbands, love your wives, just as Christ also loved the church and gave Himself for her."*

Investing in Spiritual Growth

Establishing priorities includes intentional investment in spiritual growth both individually and collectively as a family. Engaging in regular devotional practices, attending church services, and studying the Bible together foster a deepening connection with God. Psalm 1:2-3 vividly portrays those prioritising God's Word: *"But his delight is in the law of the Lord, and in His law he meditates day and night. He shall be like a tree planted by the rivers of water, that brings forth its fruit in its season."*

Saying "No" to Distractions

In the pursuit of God-centred priorities, discernment plays a vital role in recognising and saying "no" to distractions that divert focus from what truly matters. Setting boundaries with technology, media, and commitments that hinder spiritual growth and quality family time becomes imperative.

Cultivating a Heart of Service

Prioritising service and ministry as a family extends the impact of God-centred priorities beyond the walls of the home. Engaging in acts of kindness, community service, and outreach not only embodies the teachings of Jesus but also nurtures a sense of purpose and compassion in young hearts.

Flexibility and Adaptability

While establishing priorities is crucial, life's unpredictability requires a dose of flexibility and openness to adaptation. Embracing the truth of James 4:15, *"Instead you ought to say, 'If the Lord wills, we shall live and do this or that,'"* families recognise that God's guidance takes precedence over rigid plans.

Cultivating a Legacy of God-Centred Living

As young families set God-centred priorities, they contribute to a legacy transcending time. Prioritising God's presence, love, and values ensures that the family's journey is marked by purpose, fulfilment, and the eternal impact of living in alignment with His design.

In the beautiful symphony of life, establishing God-centred priorities becomes a melodic rhythm that harmonises faith, relationships, personal growth, and the pursuit of meaningful goals. Young families, guided by the principles of faith, prayer, and intentional choices, embark on a journey of purpose and fulfilment. This journey resonates with God's heart and resonates through the generations.

Focus on a Few Basic Objectives

Amid life's bustling complexities, focusing on a few core objectives holds significant wisdom. Imagine life as a vast landscape filled with numerous tasks, responsibilities, and commitments—each vying for our attention. It's easy to feel overwhelmed by the sheer volume of demands that life places upon us. This is where the principle of concentrating on a handful of fundamental objectives comes into play.

When we deliberately narrow our focus to a select set of key objectives, we harness the power of simplicity and clarity. Instead of being scattered in various directions, we align our efforts toward what truly matters. This focused approach allows us to effectively channel our energy, time, and resources, ensuring that we allocate them to pursuits that resonate deeply with our values and goals.

We create a sense of purposeful direction by identifying and prioritising these core objectives. Rather than being swept away by the ceaseless stream of demands, we chart a deliberate course that leads us closer to our desired outcomes. This sense of purpose is a guiding compass, helping us make decisions that align with our overarching goals and aspirations.

Moreover, concentrating on a few primary objectives aids us in managing the often overwhelming nature of modern life. The rapid pace of technology, the influx of information, and the myriad of responsibilities can easily leave us feeling stretched thin. However, when we intentionally focus on a select few priorities, we cultivate a sense of control over our lives. We become better equipped to handle the various challenges and tasks that come our way because we have a clear framework for evaluating their importance and relevance.

In essence, this approach is about quality over quantity. It's not about attempting to do everything or appeasing every demand that arises. Instead, investing our time and energy into pursuits that align with our values, aspirations, and long-term vision is a deliberate choice. This intentional focus allows us to achieve mastery and fulfilment in our endeavours as we dedicate ourselves to tasks that truly matter to us.

In conclusion, the notion that focusing on a few essential objectives enhances our ability to manage life's demands is a powerful reminder of the importance of intentional living. By discerning what truly matters to us and channelling our efforts toward those objectives, we simplify our lives, cultivate a sense of purpose, and find greater fulfilment amid life's ever-changing landscape.

As we reflect on the importance of Embracing Contentment and Establishing Priorities for a Balanced Life, we embark on a profound journey of self-discovery and purpose. Chapter 27 delves into the intricate process of Unveiling Your Life's Purpose: Crafting a Symphony of Destiny. Just as a composer meticulously weaves notes together to create a symphony, we too can craft our life's purpose in harmony with God's divine plan. Join us as we explore the path to uncovering our unique purpose and how it contributes to the beautiful melody of God's overarching design.

Chapter 27

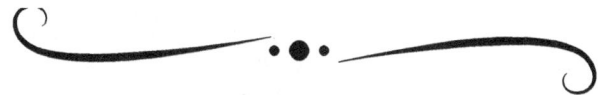

Unveiling Your Life's Purpose: Crafting a Symphony of Destiny

Story: The Weaver's Legacy

In a quaint village nestled between rolling hills, lived an elderly woman named Eliza. She was known far and wide for her exceptional weaving skills. Her hands, weathered by time, held a lifetime of stories within each thread she wove.

Eliza's granddaughter, Emily, was captivated by her grandmother's craft. She spent countless afternoons watching Eliza's skilled hands turn threads into intricate patterns. One day, as Emily observed her grandmother weaving, she couldn't contain her curiosity any longer. "Grandmother, how do you decide which colours to use and where to place them?"

Eliza smiled and beckoned Emily to sit beside her. "My dear, each thread represents a part of life—a moment, an experience, a dream. Just as God weaves the threads of our lives into a beautiful tapestry, I choose colours that reflect the varied seasons of life."

Emily's eyes sparkled with wonder. "But how do you know where to place each thread?"

Eliza's eyes twinkled with wisdom. "Ah, that's the heart of weaving, my child. I don't always know in advance. I trust the pattern will emerge as I weave, guided by my years of experience and the vision in my heart."

As Emily grew, she continued to learn from her grandmother. When Eliza's hands could no longer weave, she handed Emily a loom and a collection of colourful threads. "It's your turn now, my dear. Weave your own tapestry—one that reflects your purpose, your dreams, and the legacy you want to leave behind."

Years passed, and Emily's weaving skills flourished. She created tapestries that told stories of joy, challenges, growth, and love. Each thread represented a choice, a decision, and a moment of alignment with her purpose. As she weaved, Emily realised that her life was a tapestry, and every experience was a thread carefully woven by the Creator.

One day, a young child visited Emily's studio and marvelled at her tapestries. "How do you know where to place each thread?" the child asked.

Emily smiled, just as her grandmother had once smiled at her. "My dear, life is like weaving. Each thread holds a purpose, and as we align with God's design, a beautiful tapestry of fulfilment is revealed."

The child's eyes shone with understanding, and as they left, Emily looked at her work—the tapestries that embodied a life of purpose, fulfilment, and divine alignment. Just like Eliza had passed down her legacy, Emily was now passing down the wisdom of purpose to the next generation, weaving a tapestry of love, guidance, and enduring significance.

Imagine life as a symphony, where each note and melody contribute to a harmonious masterpiece. Just as a composer carefully orchestrates each element, so does the Creator weave the fabric of our lives with purpose and intention? This chapter invites young families to embark on a profound journey that uncovers the unique purpose embedded within their hearts, resonating with the divine rhythm of existence.

The Quest of the Heart

At the heart of every individual lies a quest—a yearning to unveil the purpose that infuses life with meaning. It's a quest that aligns with the Creator's design, as Jeremiah 29:11 (NKJV) assures us: "For I know the thoughts that I think toward you, says the Lord, thoughts of peace and not of evil, to give you a future and a hope." Families are urged to engage in soulful dialogues, exploring their passions, talents, and aspirations to unlock the door to their God-given purpose.

Story: The Potter's Vision

Step into a timeless pottery studio where a skilled craftsman transforms shapeless clay into exquisite vessels. Young David, an observer, asks the potter, "How do you shape something so formless into art?" The potter responds with a knowing smile, "I see its potential beyond the surface. Likewise, God, the Divine Potter, crafts each life with purpose, shaping us for His masterpiece." This encounter leaves an indelible mark on David's heart, forever reminding him of his unique purpose within the grand design.

Harmonising with Divine Design

As families embark on the journey of purpose, they set sail towards aligning their lives with the Creator's design. Romans 12:2 resonates as a guiding beacon: *"And do not be conformed to this world, but be transformed by the renewing of your mind, that you may prove what is that good and acceptable and perfect will of God."* Through prayer, introspection, and seeking guidance from mentors, families chart a course that resonates with the symphony of God's intentions.

Echoes of Impact

Purpose reverberates beyond individual lives; it extends its notes into the world around us. Families are invited to see their purpose not only as a personal journey but also as a collective impact. Galatians 6:10 underscores this call: *"Therefore, as we have opportunity, let us do good to all, especially to those who are of the household of faith."* Families become instruments of change by harmonising their purpose with acts of compassion, service, and love.

Navigating the Crescendos of Challenge

The journey of purpose isn't without its crescendos of challenges. Just as Jesus faced trials during His mission, families, too, encounter obstacles that refine their purpose. Romans 8:28 offers reassurance: *"And we know that all things work together for good to those who love God, to those who are the called according to His purpose."* In these challenges, families find strength, resilience, and a deepening connection to their purpose.

A Symphony of Fulfilment with God

Within the tapestry of purpose lies the ultimate fulfilment—our connection with God. Psalm 37:4 illuminates this truth: *"Delight yourself also in the Lord, and He shall give you the desires of your heart."* As families align their purpose with divine delight, they uncover the deepest satisfaction—the joy of walking hand in hand with the Creator.

A Symphony of Destiny

In the quest for purpose, families discover the notes that compose the symphony of their lives. Each chapter uncovers a melody, every challenge adds depth, and each act of kindness amplifies the harmonious resonance of their existence. As they align with the Creator's divine composition, their lives become remarkable symphonies echoing through time.

May these pages be filled with the symphonic journey of self-discovery that unravels the melodies within their souls. With hearts attuned to divine guidance and a spirit open to purpose, may young families not only find their unique notes in the grand symphony but also leave an eternal imprint on the tapestry of creation.

As we conclude our exploration of unveiling life's purpose and the intricate symphony of destiny that each young Christian family contributes to, we find ourselves drawn to a fundamental virtue that resonates deeply with the essence of harmonious living. Just as a symphony requires the harmonious interplay of various instruments to create a melodious masterpiece, so does the journey of a Christian family demand the art of compromise—a symphony of unity and shared objectives.

Chapter 28: The Art of Compromise: Harmonising Objectives with Unity Within the tapestry of family life, where diverse personalities, aspirations, and dreams converge, the art of compromise emerges as a guiding principle that echoes Christ's call to unity and humility. In this chapter, we delve into the profound significance of compromise in nurturing healthy relationships, fostering understanding, and prioritising collective well-being.

Compromise, often misunderstood as a sign of weakness, is, in truth, a demonstration of strength—a willingness to embrace humility and esteem others above oneself. By exploring biblical insights, drawing wisdom from early church fathers like John Chrysostom and Pope Shenouda III, and extending these principles to children from a young age, we'll unravel the transformative power of compromise in building Christ-centred families.

The scriptures remind us of the Apostle Paul's words in Philippians 2:3-4: *"Let nothing be done through selfish ambition or conceit, but in lowliness of mind let each esteem others better than himself. Let each of you look out not only for his own interests, but also for the interests of others."* These verses encapsulate the essence of compromise—a virtue that transcends personal preferences in pursuit of unity and shared objectives.

Join us in Chapter 28 as we navigate the art of compromise, discovering its profound impact on relationships, parenting, and communal living. Just as our Creator orchestrates the symphony of the universe, so too can we harmonise our individual objectives within the context of Christian love, creating a melodious arrangement that echoes the heart of Christ Himself."

With this link, you can effectively transition from exploring life's purpose and destiny to the theme of compromise and its importance in fostering unity and shared objectives within young Christian families.

Chapter 28

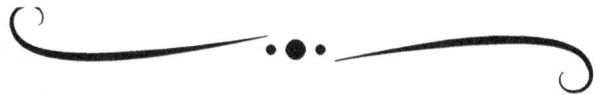

The Art of Positive Compromise to Focus on a Few Basic Objectives

The Brief Journey

Once upon a train ride, a wise man found himself on a journey. At a station, a young man with an air of impatience joined him, his numerous bags crashing into the older man as he settled in without consideration.

Witnessing this scene, my heart brimmed with discontent, and I couldn't help but inquire why the sage hadn't reproached the disruptive youth. With a gentle smile, the wise man replied, "There's no need to be stern or engage in quarrels over trifles. The journey is short, and my stop awaits at the next station."

"The journey is short" – those words resonated deeply within me. They seemed deserving of being inscribed in liquid gold, a principle to be embraced and woven into our

The Balance Beam

daily lives. Indeed, there's no need to be harsh and contentious about every matter. Instead, let us be quick to forgive, for our journey is but fleeting.

If each of us takes to heart the brevity of our sojourn – as the priest prays and recites during the commemoration in the Holy Liturgy - in this world, we'll eschew needless arguments and extend forgiveness readily, whether in abundance or scarcity. We'll abstain from grand or minuscule squabbles and choose to pardon rather than resent. Our manners will be kind, and gratitude will flow towards the blessings bestowed upon us.

If someone shatters your heart and departs from your expectations, maintain composure; the journey is short.

Stay calm if betrayed, deceived, or ridiculed; the journey is short.

Regardless of the injustices endured at the hands of others, remain tranquil; the journey is short.

Should one forget your extended kindness, stay composed; the journey is short.

Stay serene when your rights are belittled or unappreciated; the journey is short.

If your child's scholastic achievements fall short, stay composed; the journey is short.

May our hearts brim with love and serenity. Our journey is fleeting, irreversible once its end arrives. None can predict the duration of their voyage or whether they'll reach the next station. The journey is short... truly, remarkably brief.

Do you know what is the key word in the above story? That man mastered the **art of compromise!**

In the vibrant tapestry of life, where diverse perspectives and desires interweave, the art of compromise emerges as a cornerstone of healthy relationships and harmonious living. At its core, compromise is the bridge that connects differing viewpoints, fostering understanding, unity, and mutual growth. In this chapter, we embark on a journey to explore the profound significance of compromise, drawing insights from Scripture, the teachings of early church fathers, and the wisdom of contemporary Christian leaders.

Understanding the Essence of Compromise:

Compromise, often misunderstood as a sign of weakness and always carries a tinge of negative connotation, is actually a demonstration of strength—a willingness to prioritise unity and shared objectives over individual preferences. It is a virtue that reflects the humility and selflessness taught by Christ and exemplified by His apostles. The Apostle Paul's wisdom in Philippians 2:3-4 (NKJV) provides a profound guiding principle: "Let nothing be done through selfish ambition or conceit, but in lowliness of mind let each esteem others better than himself. Let each of you look out not only for his own interests, but also for the interests of others."

This divine wisdom from Saint Paul underscores the foundation of the art of compromise. It speaks to the heart of humility—a recognition that the needs and desires of others are just as valuable as our own. In a world that often celebrates individualism and self-centeredness, the call to esteem others above ourselves challenges us to embrace a higher standard of interaction—one that prioritises the community's well-being over personal gain.

Early church fathers also recognised the transformative power of humility and the virtue of compromise. Saint John Chrysostom, a revered voice of early Christianity, commented on humility's role in compromise, saying, "Humility is the root, mother, nurse, foundation, and bond of all virtue. We are born of it, we live by it, and it leads us to heavenly life." Chrysostom's insight resonates with Paul's teaching, highlighting humility as the cornerstone of a life characterised by compromise.

As we go deeper into the essence of compromise, we are reminded that it mirrors Christ's own self-sacrificial nature. Jesus, in His life and ultimate sacrifice on the cross, exemplified the epitome of humility and selflessness. Pope Shenouda III emphasised this connection. He stated, *"Compromise is a virtue that maintains unity in the family and builds love."* This sentiment echoes Christ's teachings of loving one another as He loved us, which inherently involves putting others' needs and interests before our own.

In the art of compromise, we not only seek to find common ground but also create an environment where empathy, understanding, and unity flourish. It is a conscious choice to bridge gaps, dissolve conflicts, and foster an atmosphere where the Kingdom values of selflessness, love, and humility are upheld. Just as Christ's sacrificial love reconciled humanity with God, our willingness to compromise can reconcile differences and build bonds within families and communities. It's very important to highlight and distinguish between areas and times we need to compromise and others we never compromise!

In the tapestry of life, compromise emerges as a vibrant thread that weaves diverse perspectives and desires into a harmonious whole. It reflects the essence of Christ's teachings, the wisdom of the Apostle Paul, and the insights of early church fathers. As young Christian families embrace the art of compromise, they embrace the spirit of Christ, demonstrating strength through humility and fostering unity through selflessness. Through compromise, families not only navigate the challenges of life but also model a Christ-centred way of living—one that resonates with the call to love our neighbours as ourselves and to prioritise the interests of others.

Biblical Insights on Compromise:

Throughout the Bible, we encounter instances where compromise is pivotal in resolving conflicts and achieving collective goals. One notable example is the story of Abraham and Lot in Genesis 13:8-9, where Abraham suggests a compromise to prevent discord: *"Please let there be no strife between you and me... Is not the whole land before you? Please separate from me. If you take the left, then I will go to the right; or, if you go to the right, then I will go to the left."*

In this account, Abraham's nephew Lot and his own household had grown so numerous that the land they inhabited could no longer sustain them both. This scarcity led to strife between their respective herdsmen. Recognising the potential harm that discord could cause to their relationship and the unity of their families, Abraham takes the initiative to propose a compromise.

Abraham's approach reflects the principles of humility and selflessness at the core of compromise. Instead of demanding his own way or asserting his rights, Abraham seeks a peaceful solution that benefits both parties. His willingness to yield his own preferences demonstrates his commitment to prioritising harmony and unity over personal gain.

This story resonates with the teachings of early church fathers as well. Saint John Chrysostom, known for his wisdom and insight, stated, *"For God grants more to those who are willing to give up their rights."* This echoes Abraham's voluntarily relinquishing his preferences to ensure peace and unity.

As we examine the art of compromise within the context of young Christian families, the story of Abraham and Lot offers valuable lessons. It underscores that compromise is not a sign of weakness but a sign of strength—a strength rooted in humility and a desire to uphold unity. Conflict and disagreements are inevitable in the family unit due to diverse personalities, perspectives, and preferences. However, in these moments, the art of compromise can shine as a beacon of Christ-like behaviour.

In the context of teaching this virtue to children from a young age, the story of Abraham and Lot can serve as a powerful example. Parents can share this story with their children, emphasising the importance of valuing harmony and considering the needs of others. By using relatable language and scenarios, parents can help children grasp the concept of compromise and its significance in building healthy relationships.

Through this biblical account, children can understand that compromise is not about surrendering one's values or beliefs but finding common ground that promotes understanding and unity. Parents can encourage their children to think about situations where they can apply the principle of compromise—whether it's sharing toys, deciding on family activities, or resolving conflicts with siblings or friends.

Incorporating early church fathers' teachings into this lesson, parents can highlight the virtue of humility and how it aligns with the spirit of compromise. Children can learn that compromise is not just a practical solution to conflicts but a reflection of Christ's teachings and an expression of love for others.

In conclusion, Abraham and Lot's story is a timeless illustration of the art of compromise. It showcases the strength of humility, the power of unity, and the importance of prioritising harmony over personal desires. By weaving this story into the fabric of young Christian families' lives and incorporating the wisdom of early church fathers, parents can instil the value of compromise in their children from a young age. As families learn to navigate conflicts with a spirit of humility and unity, they embrace a Christ-centred approach to living—a powerful testimony of their faith and a shining example of the art of compromise.

Wisdom from the Early Church Fathers:

The wisdom of early church fathers further illuminates the virtue of compromise. Saint John Chrysostom, known for his eloquent teachings, emphasises the importance of humility in compromise. He states, *"It is impossible for one who is humble to be quarrelsome, impatient, or arrogant."* Compromise is an expression of that humility, as it acknowledges the value of another's perspective.

Applying Compromise to Young Christian Families:

Extending the practice of compromise to young Christian families is paramount for nurturing healthy relationships and instilling foundational values in children. By modelling compromise within family dynamics, parents teach their children the art of empathy, respect, and mutual consideration. The wisdom of Pope Shenouda III echoes this sentiment as he shares, *"Compromise is a foundation of strong relationships... It is a virtue that maintains unity in the family and builds love."*

Educating Children in the Art of Compromise:

Teaching children about compromise from a young age is a powerful way to cultivate a spirit of harmony and cooperation. Parents can engage children in age-appropriate discussions about the value of considering others' opinions and finding common ground. This education equips children with skills beyond the family setting, preparing them to navigate friendships, school environments, and future relationships with a spirit of compromise.

When not to compromise?

Regrettably, the art of compromise has often been misapplied throughout history, leading to significant consequences. This pattern of compromise is not limited to any specific era; instead, it spans time, and even Scripture bears witness to instances where individuals, including devoted servants of God, chose compromise over steadfastness.

In exploring these accounts, we unveil the unfortunate outcomes that can arise from compromising core principles:

Adam's Compromise: The earliest example takes us back to the Garden of Eden, where Adam chose to compromise God's command by yielding to his wife's persuasion. This compromise led to the loss of paradise, as he partook in the forbidden fruit and suffered its consequences (Genesis 3:6, 22-24). **Never compromise with sin.**

Abraham's Truth-Bending: Even the father of faith, Abraham, faced the temptation to compromise the truth. Fearing for his safety, he deceived others about his relationship with Sarah, almost resulting in the loss of his wife (Genesis 12:10-12). **Never compromise the truth.**

Sarah's Impatience: Sarah, too, succumbed to compromise when she allowed her impatience to override God's promise. She encouraged Abraham to have a child with her maidservant Hagar, leading to strained relationships and future conflicts (Genesis 16:1-12). **Never compromise your faith and God's promises.**

The Art of Positive Compromise to Focus on a Few Basic Objectives

Moses' Lapse in Obedience: despite his leadership role, Moses faced a moment of compromise when he struck the rock in anger instead of following God's command to speak to it. This compromise cost him the privilege of entering the Promised Land (Numbers 20:7-12). **Never compromise your obedience to God and His commandments.**

Samson's Weakened Devotion: The story of Samson reveals the consequences of compromising one's devotion. He allowed his heart to stray from his Nazirite vow, ultimately leading to his physical and spiritual downfall (Judges 16:4-31). **Never compromise your Christian values and promises to God.**

Israel's Departure from God's Ways: The nation of Israel repeatedly compromised God's commands, leading to their downfall and the loss of the Ark of the Covenant in battle. Their compromise with sin and idolatry resulted in exile and the loss of their homeland (1 Samuel 4:11; 2 Chronicles 36:14-17). **Never compromise with sinful thoughts or lustful desires.**

Saul's Partial Obedience: King Saul's compromise with God's command to destroy all the spoils of war demonstrated the dangers of partial obedience. His actions cost him his kingship and God's favour (1 Samuel 15:3, 20-28). **Never compromise your obedience and faithfulness to God.**

David's Moral Lapse: The beloved King David, known for his strong faith, faltered when he compromised his moral standards. His affair with Bathsheba and the subsequent murder of Uriah led to severe consequences, including the death of their infant son (2 Samuel 11:1-4; 2 Samuel 12:7-14).

Solomon's Marital Choices: King Solomon's pursuit of foreign wives for political alliances led to compromise in his faith and values. His actions divided the kingdom and resulted in loss (1 Kings 11:1-8).

Judas' Betrayal: Judas Iscariot's betrayal of Christ for monetary gain serves as a tragic example of compromising one's devotion to worldly desires. His actions resulted in eternal separation from Christ (Matthew 26:20-25, 47-49; 27:1-5).

Peter's Denial and Later Compromise: Even the apostle Peter faced moments of compromise. His denial of Christ highlighted a lapse in conviction. Later, he compromised the truth to appease the Judaizers, losing personal freedom (Mark 14:66-72; Galatians 2:11-14).

Ananias and Sapphira's Deception: In the early Christian community, Ananias and Sapphira compromised the truth by lying about their giving. Their deception led to their untimely deaths, emphasising the gravity of their compromise (Acts 5:1-11).

These accounts from Scripture remind us that compromising core principles can lead to dire consequences. While recognising the imperfections of biblical figures, we can draw lessons from their choices. The thread that weaves through these stories is the importance of upholding God's truth and adhering to His ways. May these lessons guide us as we navigate the complexities of our own lives, always seeking to stand firm in our faith and values.

Establishing Objectives within Compromise:

While compromise involves finding a middle ground, it's essential to establish overarching objectives. This means identifying core values, goals, and principles that guide compromise. For Christian families, these objectives may be rooted in Scripture, such as promoting love, unity, and selflessness. Through the lens of compromise, families can work together to achieve these higher goals while embracing individual differences.

In conclusion, the art of compromise is a dynamic dance that unites differing viewpoints, nurtures unity, and empowers young Christian families to pursue shared objectives. Families can navigate the delicate balance between individual desires and collective harmony by incorporating principles from Scripture, the teachings of early church fathers, and the wisdom of contemporary Christian leaders. As parents impart the value of compromise to their children, they equip the next generation with an invaluable tool for building strong relationships and contributing to a world grounded in understanding and love.

Chapter 29

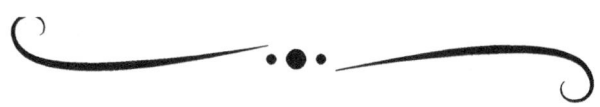

The Laws of in-laws

I recall the early years of my marriage when my wife and I often grappled with specific issues, especially during festive seasons and celebrations. Questions like, "Where should we spend Christmas Eve or Christmas Day?" Moreover, considerations surrounding birthdays frequently come up.

Coming from diverse backgrounds with varying social circles, traditions, and habits, and standing at different points on the spectrum of spirituality, maturity, wisdom, love, and willingness to compromise sometimes felt like navigating a complex maze. These differences could become fertile ground for disagreements, conflicts, and even marital quarrels. And, to add to the complexity, there were occasional crosswinds from less mature parents and in-laws.

It was a learning journey to blend our unique perspectives, appreciate each other's backgrounds, and find common ground while dealing with external pressures.

Often, we hear couples express their frustrations with in-law relationships. Issues such as control, interference, inconvenience, and clashes of values and traditions are shared. Let's explore how to address these challenges and build healthy relationships with our parents and in-laws.

"My wife's parents give her money to buy things we can't afford. I resent that. I wish they would let us run our own lives." "My husband's parents just 'drop in' unannounced. Sometimes, I'm in the middle of a project I must complete. I wish they would respect our schedules." It's not uncommon to encounter such situations in confessions from young couples. On the flip side, we also hear from in-laws and parents who may tend to overstep their bounds and interfere in their children's lives. These scenarios highlight the delicate balance couples often need to strike when managing relationships with their parents and spouses.

In-law problems are common and often include such issues as control, interference, inconvenience and the clashing of values and traditions. Separating from parents, Scripture indicates two parallel guidelines for relating to parents after marriage.

First, we are to separate from our parents.

"Therefore a man shall leave his father and his mother and hold fast to his wife, and they shall become one flesh" (Genesis 2:24). God's pattern for marriage involves "leaving" parents and "holding fast" to a husband or wife. Thus, marriage brings a change of allegiance. Before marriage, one's allegiance is to one's parents; after marriage, allegiance shifts to one's partner. For example, if there is a conflict of interest between a man's wife and his mother, the husband must stand with his wife. This does not mean that the mother is to be treated unkindly.

It means that she is no longer the dominant female in his life. No couple will reach their full potential in marriage without this psychological break from their parents. This principle of separation is perhaps most important in decision-making. Your parents and in-laws may have suggestions about many aspects of your married life. These should be taken into consideration. However, you must make your own decisions as a couple. It's important that you not allow parents to manipulate you into deciding on which the two of you do not agree.

Honouring parents

The second fundamental principle of marriage is to honour our parents (Exodus 20:12). This command does not cease when we are married. The word honour means to show respect. It involves treating others with kindness and dignity. One wife said, "My parents do not live respectable lives. How can I respect them when I disagree with their actions?" Not all parents live honourable lives. Their actions may not be worthy of respect, but because of their unique God-given role in our lives, it is always right to honour our parents and our spouse's parents. How do we express honour to our parents in daily life? By keeping the lines of communication open — visiting, telephoning. Such communication conveys the message, "I still love you and want you to be a part of my life." Failure to communicate says, in effect, "I no longer care." Building mutual respect Leaving and honouring sets the stage for a relationship of mutual respect with parents and in-laws. Even so, this kind of relationship doesn't always come easily. Let me suggest four areas that may require extra diligence as you seek to establish respect:

Holiday traditions

Christmas is the biggie. His parents and your parents want you at their house on Christmas Day. Unless they live beside each other, that will likely be impossible. So, you must negotiate a settlement that will be fair and show respect to both parents. That may mean Christmas with his parents and Easter with her parents, with the understanding that you will switch the order next year. Or it may mean that the two of you decide to establish your own Christmas traditions and not visit either set of parents. However, this second choice will likely be taken as a symbol of disrespect — at least until you have children.

Religious differences

Seldom do two individuals come to marriage with the same spiritual background. They may both be Christians but come from different doctrinal traditions. Parents can have strong beliefs that may differ from yours or your spouse's. Not all religious beliefs could possibly be true — they may even contradict each other. But we must show respect and give each other the same freedom God grants us. When you respect religious differences, you create a positive relationship in which you can discuss religious issues openly. You may even learn something from one another.

Privacy

A young husband said, "We really need help with my mom and dad. We don't want to hurt them, but we have got to do something. We never know when they will drop by for a visit, and sometimes it's really inconvenient. "In fact, last week, my wife and I agreed that we would get the children to bed early and have an extended time together. By 8 o'clock, the children were asleep when suddenly the doorbell rang, and my mother and father were there. As you can imagine, it destroyed our dreams of a romantic evening." I told the young husband that his parents were not respecting his privacy. "I know," he said, "but we don't know what to do about it." "Let me suggest you talk with your father privately and tell him what happened last week," I said. "If you share what happened, chances are, he will explain it to your mother, and they will begin to call before they come over." I saw the couple a few months later, and the wife said, thanks so much. His mother got upset for about three weeks and didn't come to visit at all. Then we talked about it and assured them they were always welcome but explained that it was helpful if they would call and ask if it was convenient. We haven't had any problems since then." Many couples wait until they are so frustrated with their in-laws that they lash out with harsh and condemning words and fracture the relationship. But when we speak with respect, we are likely to get respect.

Differing opinions and ideas

Scripture indicates that we ought to seek the counsel of others to make wise decisions (Proverbs 11:14; 19:20). Your in-laws may have more experience and wisdom than you — at least in certain areas of life. So, ask for their advice. Then, make the decision that you and your spouse think is wise. Our political, religious, and philosophical ideas are often different from those held by our in-laws, so don't think you must always agree with their ideas. But we can enrich one another's lives when we share our thoughts and reflect on what the other person shares. We can respect their ideas even though we may disagree with them: "I hear what you're saying, and I think it makes sense from one perspective. But let me share my perspective." Because you have listened, he or she will more likely listen to your idea. Then, each of you can evaluate what was said. A different perspective can help us refine our own ideas into a more meaningful approach to life, and respect for each other can be foundational to a healthy in-law relationship.

In-law relationships can be challenging, but when approached with respect and open communication in a Christian way, they can become a source of support and growth for your marriage."

Open communication is crucial when discussing relationships with parents and can help avoid fights or conflicts. Here are some tips to maintain a healthy and productive conversation:

1. **Choose the Right Time and Place:** Don't bring up sensitive topics amid a busy or stressful day. Find a quiet, relaxed time to sit down and talk. Avoid the one million dollar famous mistake, the spontaneous statement that we sometimes vomit without holding back during the heat of the moment...

2. **Use "I" Statements:** Express your feelings and concerns using "I" statements rather than "you" statements. For example, say, "I feel overwhelmed when..." instead of "You always make me feel..."

3. **Listen Actively:** Give your spouse your full attention when speaking. Avoid interrupting, and try to understand their perspective before responding.

4. **Stay Calm:** Take a break if the conversation becomes heated. Step away for a few minutes to cool off before returning to the discussion.

5. **Be Empathetic:** Try to understand your spouse's point of view, even if you disagree. Show empathy and validate their feelings.

6. **Avoid Blame:** Instead of blaming each other or your parents, focus on the issues or situations causing concern. Address the problem rather than making it about personal faults.
7. **Find Common Ground:** Seek areas of agreement and build on them. Finding common ground can help you work together to find solutions.
8. **Compromise:** Be willing to make compromises. Remember that you're a team and must find solutions that work for your marriage.
9. **Seek Guidance:** If you find it challenging to communicate without fighting, consider seeking help from a marriage counsellor or therapist. They can provide strategies for effective communication.
10. **Stay Solution-Focused:** Keep the conversation focused on finding solutions to the issues at hand. Avoid rehashing past arguments or unrelated topics.
11. **Set Boundaries Together:** When discussing boundaries with parents, decide together what limits you want to set and why. Ensure you both understand and agree on these boundaries before communicating them to your parents.
12. **Practice Patience:** Remember that open communication takes time to develop. Be patient with each other as you work on improving your communication skills.

Ultimately, open communication aims to strengthen your relationship and address concerns together as a team. By maintaining a respectful and empathetic approach, you can minimise conflicts and find constructive solutions to the challenges of dealing with parents.

Chapter 30

The Pressure of Maintaining Social Image

In pursuing faith, family, and a successful career, many young Christian families grapple with a hidden adversary: the pressure to maintain a specific social image. This external pressure, often driven by societal expectations and perceptions, can inadvertently strain marriages and financial stability.

In today's modern age of social media and ever-connected lifestyles, the pressure to maintain a particular social image has become increasingly pronounced. Also, the tendency of everyone to compare with others competitively sometimes increases the weight of the issue.

The Weight of Appearances

In today's world, appearances often carry significant weight. It's not uncommon for individuals and families to feel compelled to present a picture-perfect image to society. This pressure can manifest in various ways, from the type of house one lives in, the car one drives, to the schools their children attend. While striving for excellence is admirable, it can sometimes evolve into an unhealthy obsession with appearances.

The Subtle Tyranny of Social Comparison

While innate to human nature, social comparison has reached new heights in our digital age. Platforms like Instagram, Facebook, and TikTok often present curated snapshots of seemingly perfect lives. Young families, exposed to these polished images daily, can fall into the trap of comparison. The desire to keep up with others, or even outdo them, can lead to the relentless pursuit of material success. The allure of social validation, driven by the number of likes, shares, and comments on posts, can be deceiving. The desire to keep up with or surpass peers in the digital realm can trigger a relentless pursuit of material success and an unending quest to project an image of perfection. This, in turn, leads to an unspoken societal expectation that couples must not only excel in their careers but also exhibit their accomplishments lavishly. The psychological toll of this social image pressure cannot be underestimated. It frequently leads to anxiety, depression, and pervasive feelings of inadequacy. The constant fear of not measuring up to societal ideals can serve as a persistent source of distress, impacting not only individuals but the entire family unit.

The Struggle for Balancing Priorities

For young Christian families, balancing priorities is real and can be overwhelming. The desire to nurture a strong faith, provide a loving and stable home for their children, and excel in their careers can create tension and stress. It's not uncommon to feel torn between attending church events, spending quality time with family, and meeting work-related commitments.

Impact on Marriage: The Hidden Costs

The pressure to maintain a particular social image can strain a marriage enormously. Husbands and wives may work tirelessly to secure better incomes and financial stability, all to uphold a specific standard of living. This can lead to long working hours, increased stress, and limited quality time spent with each other and their children.

The Perceived Judgment of Others

One of the driving forces behind this pressure is the perceived judgment of others. Many individuals are preoccupied with what friends, family, colleagues, and even acquaintances might think of their lifestyle choices. This constant concern can overshadow the importance of making decisions based on one's values, priorities, and genuine needs.

Seeking Approvals and Satisfying Pride

A critical question to ponder is: Why are we caught in this unrelenting cycle of seeking social approval? At the core, are we striving to satisfy our pride and ego? Is this a means of proving our worth as parents, spouses, and individuals? Or have we unwittingly fallen into the trap of a societal image taboo, driven more by external expectations than our genuine desires and values?

The Trap of Materialism

In the pursuit of social validation, it's easy to fall into the trap of materialism. This materialistic mindset values possessions, status symbols, and outward appearances. However, it's important to remember that true happiness and fulfilment are not found in the accumulation of material wealth but in the richness of relationships, faith, and a sense of purpose.

Rediscovering Authentic Priorities

Young Christian families facing the pressure of maintaining a social image must pause and reflect on their authentic priorities. Rather than striving to meet external expectations, they should focus on nurturing their faith, strengthening family bonds, and achieving financial stability that aligns with their actual needs. Christ always addressed and focused on the need to focus on the inward man, the heart and not on the outside world with all its details and noise.

Embracing Simplicity: Liberation from the Shackles of Image

Simplicity can serve as a powerful antidote to the pressures of maintaining a social image. We should consider simplifying our lives redirecting our focus from material possessions to experiences that foster deeper connections. Embracing a simpler lifestyle can lead to financial freedom and a more balanced approach to faith, family, and work.

Overcoming the Fear of Judgment

Overcoming the fear of judgment is a pivotal step in this journey, as it involves recognising that the opinions of others do not determine one's worth. Prioritising authenticity and maintaining unwavering integrity in decision-making should always precede the fleeting validation offered by society.

In this pursuit of an authentic life centred around faith and family, one should remember the timeless wisdom of Saint Paul the Apostle, who wrote, *"But with me, it is a very small thing that I should be judged by you or by a human court"* (1 Corinthians 4:3). This verse underscores the insignificance of external judgments when compared to the greater purpose of living in accordance with one's faith and values.

As we gradually become less conscious of external opinions, we free ourselves from the unnecessary burdens of societal validation. This liberation allows us to focus our attention on what truly matters, embracing the *"glorious liberty of the children of God"* (Romans 8:21). In this newfound freedom, we discover the richness of a Christ-driven life by faith, family and authenticity, unburdened by the opinions of others, and firmly anchored in our Christian values.

Teaching Children Authentic Values

In the quest for an authentic and balanced life, passing on these values to the next generation is important. Children should be taught to prioritise faith, family, and character over material possessions. These foundational teachings will empower them to choose based on genuine values rather than external pressures. This is of utmost importance in the present times, where materialism in our lives is heavily socially infested with different teachings and values.

My blessed reader, I would like to leave you at the end of this chapter with a very famous story from the book of 1 Samuel, chapter 15, that cost King Saul a hefty price due to his poor judgment and his focus on his image.

The incident is significant in the context of discussing the pressure to maintain a certain social image and the consequences it can have.

In this story, Samuel had given Saul a specific command from God to utterly destroy the Amalekites and all their possessions as a form of divine judgment. However, when Saul and his army conquered the Amalekites, they spared King Agag's life and took some of the best livestock and plunder for themselves. When Samuel arrived to confront Saul about this disobedience, Saul attempted to justify his actions and preserve his image in front of his people.

Saul's actions in this situation highlight the powerful influence of social image and pride. He was more concerned about how his subjects would perceive him than he was about obeying God's command. His fear of losing face led him to make a series of poor decisions, ultimately resulting in God's rejection of his kingship. What a pity!

The tearing of Samuel's garment symbolises the tearing of the kingdom from Saul's hands. It signifies the gravity of Saul's disobedience and the consequences it would have on his rule and legacy. This incident is a cautionary tale about the dangers of prioritizing social image over faithfulness to God's commands. It reminds us that seeking approval and pride can lead to detrimental outcomes in our spiritual journey, just as it did for King Saul. The burden of upholding our social image can significantly affect our lives.

Conclusion

In closing, as we reflect on the journey we've taken through these 30 chapters, it's clear that the foundation of a strong Christian family is rooted in faith, love, and mutual respect. It's a foundation built upon the unwavering principles of Christ's teachings.

We've explored the challenges and joys of family life, the importance of nurturing spiritual growth in our children, and the significance of maintaining healthy marriages. We've delved into the roles of faith, prayer, and community in strengthening our families. Moreover, we've examined the pressures of maintaining a certain social image and the need to overcome them. Through it all, we've seen that at the core of it lies love - the love of God, the love within our families, and the love we extend to our church communities and beyond. May this journey serve as a reminder that, in the end, it's the love we sow and live that truly matters.

Let us continue to nurture our faith, uphold the values of our Christian families, and support one another as we journey through life together. With faith as our anchor and love as our guide, our Christian families will not only survive in today's world but thrive, becoming beacons of light in a sometimes darkened world. As we close this book, let us carry these lessons in our hearts and continue to build strong, loving, and Christ-cantered families."

Balancing faith, family, and work is challenging enough without the added pressure of maintaining a specific social image. Young Christian families should remember that their worth is not defined by possessions or appearances but by their commitment to faith, the strength of their family bonds, and their integrity in work and life decisions. By re-evaluating their priorities, embracing simplicity, and overcoming the fear of judgment, they can lead fulfilling lives that reflect their true values.

In doing so, they become a beacon of authenticity and faith in a world often preoccupied with image and materialism. The path to true contentment and peace lies in the simplicity of living according to one's convictions and cherishing the moments of love, laughter, and genuine connection with family and their Christian community. Ultimately, the authenticity of one's faith and relationships shines brightest, far outlasting the fleeting glow of social image.

Final words to thank you, my dear reader; in the intricate tapestry of life, we find ourselves woven into the grand design of faith, family, and the pursuit of God's purpose. Throughout these 30 chapters, we have explored the challenges and triumphs that young Christian families often face in their journey. We've delved into the depths of faith, the nurturing of strong Christian families, the bonds of love, the importance of community, and the pressures of maintaining a social image.

As we conclude this book, let us remember that our journey does not end here; it merely enters a new chapter. The challenges we face and the lessons we learn are not meant to be static but are part of the ever-evolving narrative of our lives.

In all of life's complexities, let us hold fast to the unchanging truths of our faith. Let us nurture our families with love and purpose, knowing they are our most precious blessings. Let us build communities that support and uplift one another, for in unity, we find strength.

But let us also release the burden of societal expectations and judgments. The fear of what others may think should not shackle us. Instead, let authenticity and integrity be our guiding stars. In the end, may our lives reflect the profound words of Saint Paul, "I have fought the good fight, I have finished the race, I have kept the faith" (2 Timothy 4:7).

With this, we embark on the next chapter of our journey, knowing that God's grace will lead us, His love will sustain us, and our faith will be our guiding light.

In closing, let us carry these principles with us, not only in our homes but also in our interactions with the world. For as we sow and live love in our families and communities, we become vessels of God's love, sharing His light with all we encounter.

May God bless your families abundantly as you embark on this beautiful and challenging journey of faith and love? Together, we can withstand the pressures of maintaining a social image and, instead, focus on the eternal values that truly matter. Let love guide you, let faith sustain you, and let mutual respect unite you, for in these, we find the strength to build strong Christian families that stand the test of time.

May your families be blessed, your faith unwavering, and your hearts filled with love. As we step forward, may we continue to grow in faith, love, and the pursuit of God's purpose, knowing that our journey is, and always will be, guided by the hand of the Almighty.

Thank you for sharing this journey with me. May God's abundant grace be with you constantly.

Fr Kyrillos Farag

www.ingramcontent.com/pod-product-compliance
Lightning Source LLC
Chambersburg PA
CBHW032037150426
43194CB00006B/314